Student Workbook

AGS Publishing
Circle Pines, MN 55014-1796
800-328-2560

© 2005 AGS Publishing
4201 Woodland Road
Circle Pines, MN 55014-1796
800-328-2560 • www.agsnet.com

AGS Publishing is a trademark and trade name of American Guidance Service, Inc.

Printed in the United States of America

ISBN 0-7854-3831-9

Product Number 93983

A 0 9 8 7 6 5 4 3 2 1

Table of Contents

Points and Lines in the Plane

EXAMPLE   Collinear points are located on the same line. Points *C, D,* and *E* are collinear.

Study the point, line, line segment, and ray.

Directions   Answer the following questions.

1. How many points are necessary to define a line? _____

2. Given three noncollinear points in space, how many lines can be drawn? _____

3. Given three collinear points in space, how many lines can be drawn? _____

4. Given three collinear points and one other point that is not on the same line, how many lines can be drawn? _____

5. How many endpoints are needed to draw four line segments? _____

6. How many endpoints are needed to draw three line segments? _____

7. How many endpoints are needed to draw six line segments? _____

8. How many endpoints are needed to draw ten line segments? _____

Directions   Tell whether each figure is a point, a line, a line segment, or a ray.

9.  _____

13.  _____

10.  _____

14. •X _____

11. •F——•G _____

15.  _____

12. •L—— _____

Measuring Line Segments

EXAMPLE   Measure a line segment by placing the zero mark of a ruler on one end and
reading the distance to the other end.

_____

The line is 4 inches long.

Directions   Measure the following line segments in inches.

1. _____

2. _____

3. _____

4. _____

5. _____

Directions   Measure the following line segments in centimeters.

6. _____

7. _____

8. _____

9. _____

10. _____

Ruler Postulates

EXAMPLE   Given line *AB*, the number line can be chosen so that *A* is at zero and *B* is a positive number.

The distance between *A* and *B* = |3 − 0| or |0 − 3|.   *AB* = 3

Directions   Use the Ruler Placement Postulate to calculate the distance between *A* and *B*.

1.
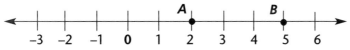
_____

2.

_____

3.

_____

4.
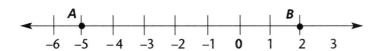
_____

EXAMPLE   If *B* is between *A* and *C*, then *AB* + *BC* = *AC*.

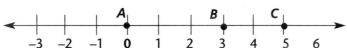

AB = 3, *BC* = 2, *AC* = 5
AB + *BC* = 3 + 2 = 5

Directions   Use the Segment Addition Postulate to prove that *B* is between *A* and *C*.

5.
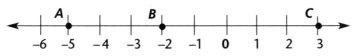
_____

Copying and Bisecting Angles

EXAMPLE   Angles can be copied exactly using a compass and straightedge.

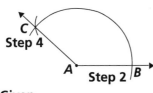   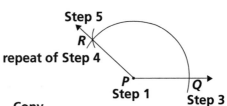

Given   Copy

Directions   Copy each angle using a compass and straightedge.

1.    2.    3.

4.   5.

EXAMPLE   Angles can be bisected exactly using a compass.

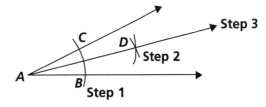

Directions   Copy each angle. Then bisect the angle you've drawn using a compass and a straightedge.

6.   7.    8.

9.   10.

Angle Measurement

EXAMPLE   Angles can be measured exactly using a protractor.

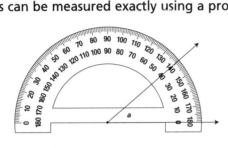

The measure of angle *a* is 40°.

Directions   Measure the following angles.

1. _____
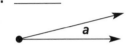

2. _____
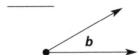

3. _____

4. _____
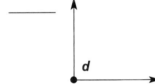

5. _____

6. _____

Directions   Classify the following angles as either *acute, right, obtuse,* or *straight.*

7. _____
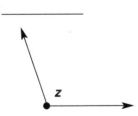

8. _____
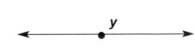

9. _____
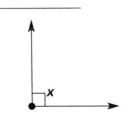

10. _____
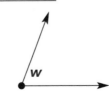

Name _____ Date _____ Period _____

Complementary and Supplementary Angles

EXAMPLE Two angles whose measures add to 90° are called complementary angles.

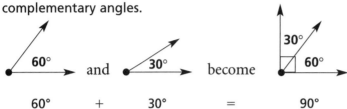

60°   +   30°   =   90°

Directions Measure the angle shown and then draw an angle that is complementary to it. Label the angle measures.

1.   **2.**   **3.**

4.   **5.**

EXAMPLE Two angles whose measures add to 180° are called supplementary angles.

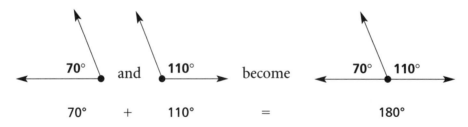

70°   +   110°   =   180°

Directions Measure the angle shown and then draw an angle that is supplementary to it. Label the angle measures.

6.   **7.**   **8.**

9.    **10.**

Algebra and Angles

EXAMPLE Solve for the missing angles.

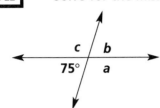

$a + 75° = 180°$ $b + 105° = 180°$ $c + 75° = 180°$
$a = 180° - 75°$ $b = 180° - 105°$ $c = 180° - 75°$
$a = 105°$ $b = 75°$ $c = 105°$

Directions Solve for the missing angles.

1. m∠r _____
   m∠s _____
   m∠t _____

2. m∠l _____
   m∠m _____
   m∠n _____

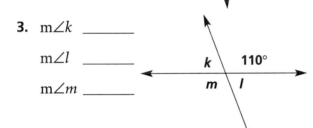

3. m∠k _____
   m∠l _____
   m∠m _____

4. m∠a _____
   m∠b _____
   m∠c _____

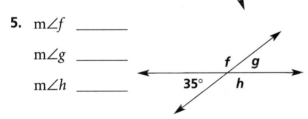

5. m∠f _____
   m∠g _____
   m∠h _____

Directions Find the measure of each numbered angle, given m∠1 = 44°.

6. m∠2 _____

7. m∠3 _____

8. m∠4 _____

9. m∠5 _____

10. m∠6 _____

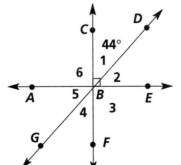

Algebra Connection: Positive Exponents

EXAMPLE   Multiply $x^3 \cdot x^4$.

To multiply expressions with the same base, add the exponents.

$x^3 \cdot x^4 = \underbrace{x \cdot x \cdot x} \cdot \underbrace{x \cdot x \cdot x \cdot x} = x^7$

$x^3 \cdot x^4 = x^{3+4} = x^7$

Directions Multiply.

1. $x^2 \cdot x^9$ _____

2. $y^{10} \cdot y^5$ _____

3. $n^8 \cdot n^3$ _____

4. $m^3 \cdot m^3 \cdot m^9$ _____

5. $a^6 \cdot a^5 \cdot a \cdot a^2$ _____

6. $r^2 \cdot s^5 \cdot r^3 \cdot s^7$ _____

EXAMPLE   Divide $a^7 \div a^3$.

To divide expressions with the same base, subtract the exponents.

$a^7 \div a^3 = \frac{a \cdot a \cdot a \cdot a \cdot a \cdot a \cdot a}{a \cdot a \cdot a} = a^{7-3} = a^4$

Directions Divide.

7. $y^8 \div y^6$ _____

8. $a^9 \div a^5$ _____

9. $b^8 \div b$ _____

10. $z^5 \div z^4$ _____

11. $n^8 \div n^3$ _____

12. $x^7 \div x^7$ _____

EXAMPLE   For what value of n is $a^7 \cdot x^4 \cdot a^3 \cdot x^2 = a^n \cdot x^6$ true?

$a^7 \cdot x^4 \cdot a^3 \cdot x^2 = a^{7+3} \cdot x^{4+2} = a^{10} \cdot x^6$

So, $a^7 \cdot x^4 \cdot a^3 \cdot x^2 = a^n \cdot x^6$ is true for $n = 10$.

Directions Find the value of n that makes each statement true.

13. $y^2 \cdot b^4 \cdot y^7 = b^4 \cdot y^n$ _____

14. $\frac{e^{11}}{e^8} = e^n$ _____

15. $a^7 \cdot b^9 \cdot a^6 = a^n \cdot b^9$ _____

16. $w^n \div w^8 = w^5$ _____

17. $r^2 \div r^n = 1$ _____

18. $p^2 \cdot r^3 \cdot p^4 \cdot r^2 = p^6 \cdot r^n$ _____

19. $\frac{y^7}{y^0} = y^n$ _____

20. $m^6 \cdot s \cdot s \cdot m^3 = m^9 \cdot s^n$ _____

Conditionals

EXAMPLE

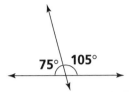

75° 105°

If <u>two angles are supplementary</u>, then ⟨the sum of their measures equals 180°.⟩

The underlined part of the conditional, or the "If" part, is the hypothesis.
The circled part of the conditional, or the "Then" part, is the conclusion.

Directions   Write *True* or *False* for each of the following conditionals.
Underline the hypothesis and circle the conclusion.

1. If an angle is less than 90°, then the angle is an acute angle.   _____

2. If two circles have the same radius, then they are equal to one another.   _____

3. If a figure has five sides, then it must contain at least one right angle.   _____

4. If a closed figure has four angles, then the sum of their measures
   must equal 360°.   _____

5. If the measure of one angle created by the intersection of two lines is 90°,
   then all four of the angles created by the intersection of the two lines will
   measure 90°.   _____

6. If your computer doesn't work when you turn it on, then there must
   be something wrong with the processor.   _____

7. If it is snowing outside, then the temperature must be less than
   32° Fahrenheit.   _____

8. If it is raining outside, then you will get wet.   _____

Directions   Use a conditional to explain each situation.

9.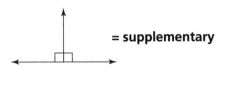

   = supplementary

10.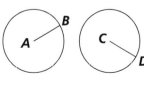

   AB = CD
   **The two circles
   are equal.**

_____   _____

_____   _____

Converses

EXAMPLE	**Given Conditional** If an angle measures > 90°, then the angle is obtuse.	**Converse** If an angle is obtuse, then it measures > 90°.

Directions Write *True* or *False* for each conditional. Then write the converse of each conditional. Write *True* or *False* for each converse.

1. If an angle is less than 90°, then it is a right angle.

_____   _____

_____   _____

2. If a circle has the same diameter as the length of the side of a square, then the circle and the square are equal.

_____   _____

_____   _____

3. If the measures of two pairs of supplementary angles are added together, then the sum will equal 360°.

_____   _____

_____   _____

4. If two circles have the same center but different-sized radii, then they are equal.

_____   _____

_____   _____

5. If the measures of all four angles of a closed four-sided figure are 90°, then the figure is a rectangle.

_____   _____

_____   _____

6. If the measures of two pairs of complementary angles are added together, then the sum is equal to the measures of two right angles.

_____   _____

_____   _____

Directions Write a conditional for each situation.

7. A conditional that is true whose converse is true

_____

8. A conditional that is false but whose converse is true

_____

9. A conditional that is true but whose converse is false

_____

10. A conditional that is false whose converse is false

_____

Lines and Euclid's Postulates

EXAMPLE

Euclid's Postulate 1	A straight line can be drawn from any point to any point.	
Euclid's Postulate 2	A finite straight line can be extended continuously in a straight line.	

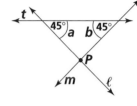

Euclid's Postulate 5 | If two lines ℓ and m are cut by a third line t, and the two inside angles, a and b, together measure less than two right angles, then the two lines ℓ and m, when extended, will meet on the same side as angles a and b.

Parallel Postulate 5 | If there is a line ℓ and a point P not on ℓ, then there is only one line that passes through P parallel to ℓ.

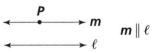

Directions Use the above postulates to make the following constructions. List the postulates you use.

1. Draw a square by connecting points A, B, C, and D.

A.   .B

D.   .C

_____

2. Draw a straight line that is parallel to line m and passes through point X. Then draw arrows showing that line m is extended continuously.

_____

3. Extend lines a and b to form an equilateral triangle.

_____

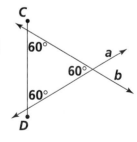

Directions Use Euclid's Postulates to tell whether the following statements are true. List which postulates were used.

4. Points A, B, and C can be joined by line segments to form a triangle.

_____

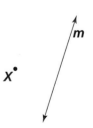

5. There is more than one line that can be parallel to line m and pass through point X.

_____

Circles and Right Angles

EXAMPLE

Euclid's Postulate 3   A circle may be described
with any center and distance.

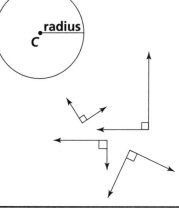

Euclid's Postulate 4   All right angles are equal to one another.

Directions   Use the above postulates to make the following constructions.
List the postulates you use.

1. Draw four circles that are equal in such a way that lines connecting the   _____
centers of the circles form a square with right angles.

2. Draw a square. Connect the corners to create four right angles.   _____

Directions   Examine the following objects. List the different figures, such as circles,
squares, and right angles, that are contained within each object's shape.
Write the postulates that you think relate to each shape's construction.

3.
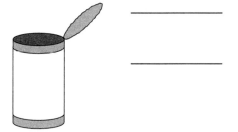
_____

_____

4.
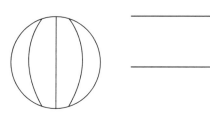
_____

_____

5.
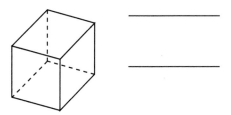
_____

_____

Using Euclid's Postulates

EXAMPLE

Given: a point *X* and a segment $\overline{CD}$
Draw a circle with *X* as the center and $\overline{CD}$ as the radius.

Euclid's Postulate 3 makes this construction possible.

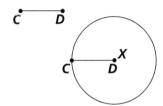

Directions Name the postulate(s) that make(s) each construction possible.

1. Draw a circle with center *A* and radius $\overline{AB}$. Then draw a circle with center *A* and a radius that is twice as long as $\overline{AB}$.

_____

2. Draw line segments connecting points *A* through *H* so that no line segment crosses another line segment.

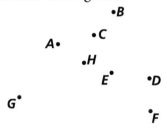

_____

3. Extend the sides of angle *a* so that four equal right angles are created.

_____

4. Draw three line segments parallel to line segment *AB* through points *X*, *Y*, and *Z*. Each line segment should be 1 centimeter shorter than $\overline{AB}$.

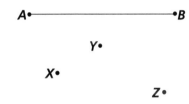

_____

5. Draw a circle with center *X* and radius $\overline{AB}$. Then draw a triangle and a square, each with sides of equal length and whose corners are a distance *AB* from *X*.

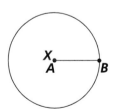

_____

Making Constructions

EXAMPLE	Draw two circles with radius *AB* and 2*AB*.

A   B
•——•

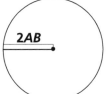

Euclid's Postulates 2 and 3 make the constructions possible.

Directions   Do these constructions on a separate sheet of paper.
Tell which postulate(s) you used to make each construction.

1. Connect all of the points
A through *H* with
all other points.

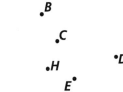

•*B*

•*C*

A•   •*H*   •*D*
        E•

                •*F*

    G•

_____

2. Given line *m* and point *S*,
draw a line that is
perpendicular to line *m*
and passes through point *S*.
Use the distance between
line *m* and point *s* as the
radius of a circle with
center *S*.

•
S

_____

3. Connect points *A*, *B*,
and *C* to form a triangle.
Then use the length
of the shortest side
as the radius to make three circles
with points *A*, *B*, and *C* as the centers.

•*A*

•
C   •
         B

_____

4. Given the line segment *AB*, draw
three different situations in which
you could extend the line segment
to include points *C* and *D*.

•*B*

•
A

_____

5. Draw two circles, one with center *M*, one with
center *N*, and each with a radius $\overline{MN}$.

_____   •
                            N
              •
              M

6. Draw four right angles equal to one another.

_____

Directions   Connect the points in each way indicated on a separate piece of paper.

7. Connect the points to create four squares.   •   •   •

8. Connect the points to create four triangles.

9. Connect the points to create two rectangles.   •   •   •

10. Connect all of the points with all of the other points.   •   •   •

Name _____ Date _____ Period _____

Axioms and Equals

EXAMPLE

Axiom 1 Things that are equal to the same thing are equal to each other.
If $a = b$ and $b = c$, then $a = c$.

Axiom 2 If equals are added to equals, the sums are equal.
If $a = b$ and $c = d$, then $a + c = b + d$.

Axiom 3 If equals are subtracted from equals, the differences are equal.
If $a = b$ and $c = d$, then $a - c = b - d$.

Directions Name the axiom that gives the reason for each step.

1. $x - 3 = 4$

$\underline{+3 = +3}$ _____

$x = 7$

2. $z + 3 = 4$

$\underline{-3 = -3}$ _____

$z = 1$

3. $y + 10 = 15$

$\underline{-10 = -10}$ _____

$y = 5$

4. $a - 75 = 76$

$\underline{+75 = +75}$ _____

$a = 151$

5. $b + c = d$

$\underline{-c = -c}$ _____

$b = d - c$

6. $b + c = d + c$

$\underline{-c = -c}$ _____

$b = d$

Directions Solve each problem to find the value of x.
List the axiom you used to solve the problem.

7. $m\angle x + m\angle y = 90°$

$m\angle x =$ _____

_____

8. $m\angle x - m\angle y = 90°$

$m\angle x =$ _____

_____

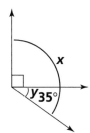

9. If $m\angle a = m\angle c$ and $m\angle b = m\angle d$, and $m\angle a + m\angle b = 180°$, and $m\angle c + m\angle d = x$, then what does x equal?

$x =$ _____ _____

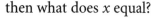

10. If $m\angle x = m\angle y + m\angle z$, and $\angle y$ is complementary with $\angle a$, and $\angle z$ is complementary with $\angle a$, and $\angle a$ is complementary with an angle whose measure is 45°, then what is the measure of $\angle x$?

$m\angle x =$ _____ _____

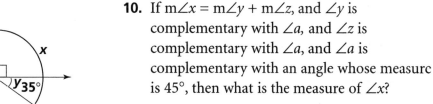

Axioms and Figures

Axiom 4   Things that are alike or coincide with one another
are equal to one another.

Axiom 5   The whole, or sum, is greater than the parts.

Directions   Answer each question. Tell which axiom you used.

1. These two figures are both complete circles with radii of 1
inch. What can you say about the two circles? Why?

_____

_____

2. This rectangle measures 1 inch long and 2 inches wide. If you
were to cut it in half along the dotted line, what could you
say about the two halves that would be created? Why?

_____

_____

3. These two triangles each have three sides that measure 1 inch
and interior angles that measure 60°. What could you say
about the two triangles? Why?

_____

_____

4. Which angles are less than 180°? Why?

_____

_____

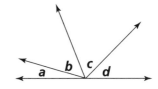

5. If you put this equilateral triangle on top of this circle so that
the circle's center was of an equal distance from each of the
triangle's corners, what could you say about the shapes created
using the triangle's corners and the circle's edge? Why?

_____

_____

Theorems

EXAMPLE   Review the theorem proving that vertical angles are equal.

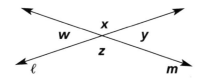

Statement	Reason
1. Lines ℓ and m intersect to form vertical $\angle x$ and $\angle z$.	1. Given.
2. $m\angle x + m\angle y = 180°$	2. $\angle x$ and $\angle y$ are adjacent on ℓ and are supplementary.
3. $m\angle y + m\angle z = 180°$	3. $\angle y$ and $\angle z$ are adjacent on ℓ and are supplementary.
4. $m\angle x + m\angle y = m\angle y + m\angle z$	4. Axiom 1, substitution, and Steps 2 and 3.
5. $\therefore\ m\angle x = m\angle z$	5. Axiom 3. If equals are subtracted from equals, the differences are equal.

Directions   Use the Vertical Angle Theorem to find the measures of angles x, y, and z.
List each step and the reason for each step.

1.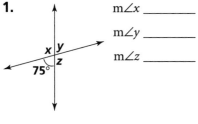

m$\angle x$ _____

m$\angle y$ _____

m$\angle z$ _____

_____

_____

2.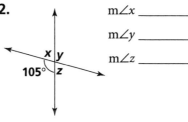

m$\angle x$ _____

m$\angle y$ _____

m$\angle z$ _____

_____

_____

3.

m$\angle x$ _____

m$\angle y$ _____

m$\angle z$ _____

_____

_____

4.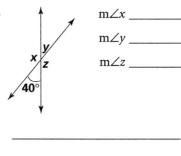

m$\angle x$ _____

m$\angle y$ _____

m$\angle z$ _____

_____

_____

5.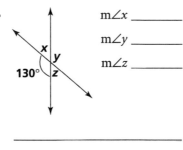

m$\angle x$ _____

m$\angle y$ _____

m$\angle z$ _____

_____

_____

Reasoning

EXAMPLE   List as many reasons as you can that prove that all four angles
          are right angles.
          1. Vertical angles are equal.
          2. Postulate 4, right angles are equal.
          3. Each of the adjacent angles to the measured right angle must
          also be a right angle because the adjacent angles are supplementary.
          Therefore, the vertical angle must also be a right angle because
          it is adjacent and supplementary to those angles.

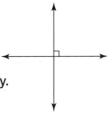

Directions   Give a reason for each of the following statements.
                 Use the diagram below.

Given: line ℓ intersects line m

1. $m\angle w = m\angle y$

2. $m\angle w < 180°$

3. $m\angle y < 180°$

4. $180° - m\angle w = 180° - m\angle y$

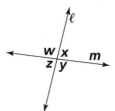

_____

_____

_____

_____

Directions   Give two different reasons for each of the following statements.
                 Use the diagram below.

Given: two lines intersect at right angles

5. $m\angle a = m\angle c$

6. $m\angle b = m\angle d$

7. $m\angle a = m\angle b = m\angle c = m\angle d$

8. $m\angle a - m\angle c = m\angle b - m\angle d$

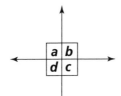

_____

_____

_____

_____

Algebra Connection: The Distributive Property

EXAMPLE	Multiply $4(x - y - 5)$.

Use the distributive property. Multiply each term inside parentheses by 4.

$4 (x - y - 5) = 4 \cdot x + 4 \cdot (-y) + 4 \cdot (-5) = 4x - 4y - 20$

Directions   Use the distributive property to multiply.

1. $4(x - y)$ _____

2. $8(2 + a)$ _____

3. $z(b - c)$ _____

4. $6(4 - p)$ _____

5. $m(13 - 2r)$ _____

6. $4(c + d + 9)$ _____

7. $m(p - q - 4)$ _____

8. $-3(x + y - 2)$ _____

9. $10(9n + 4t - m)$ _____

10. $c(x + 5b - 3r)$ _____

EXAMPLE	Factor $4x - 4y - 20$.

Step 1 Each term has a factor of 4, so 4 is a common factor of $4x$, $-4y$, and -20.

Step 2 Write each term with 4 as a factor: $4 \cdot x + 4 \cdot (-y) + 4 \cdot (-5)$

Step 3 Write the expression as the product of two terms: $4(x - y - 5)$

Directions   Factor.

11. $bx + by$ _____

12. $3a - 3b$ _____

13. $6x + 18$ _____

14. $-6x + 18$ _____

15. $3ax - 3ay$ _____

16. $bx - 5by - bz$ _____

17. $8x - 12y + 20z$ _____

18. $-9c + 6d + 21e$ _____

19. $-9c - 6d - 21e$ _____

20. $14a - 21b + 56c$ _____

Figures with Parallel Lines

EXAMPLE   Parallel lines are coplanar lines that never meet.

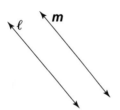

Skew lines are noncoplanar lines that never meet.

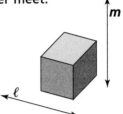

Directions   Look at each figure. Find all of the parallel lines and trace them in red. Find all of the nonparallel lines and trace them in green.

1.

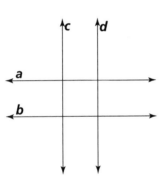

2.

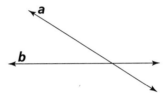

3.

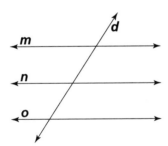

4.

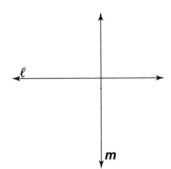

5.

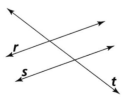

More Figures with Parallel Lines

EXAMPLE   This cube has 12 sets of parallel lines.

Directions   State how many pairs of lines are parallel in each situation.

1.   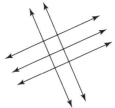   _____

2.   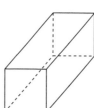   _____

3.   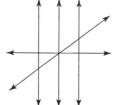   _____

4.   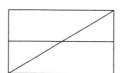   _____

Directions   Answer the following question.

5. What do you think the cube in the example would look like if all of the panels were unfolded so that the resulting image could lay flat on a table? Draw a picture to show your answer.

Transversals

EXAMPLE   Line *t* is a transversal that crosses parallel lines *ℓ* and *m*.

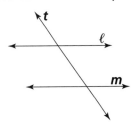

Directions   Name the transversal in each figure.

1.

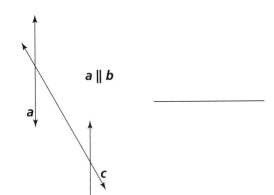

a ∥ *b*

_____

2.

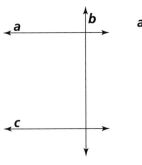

a ∥ *c*

_____

3.

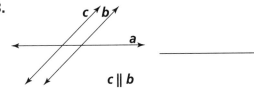

c ∥ *b*

_____

4.

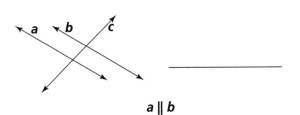

a ∥ *b*

_____

Directions   Construct two parallel lines using the two edges of your straightedge.
Draw a transversal that is not perpendicular to the parallels.
Use a protractor to measure the angles and answer the following questions.

5. Which angles appear to be equal? Which angles appear to be supplementary?

_____

More Transversals

EXAMPLE   A transversal creates eight angles. These angles
are categorized as exterior, interior, corresponding,
alternate interior, alternate exterior,
or supplementary angles.

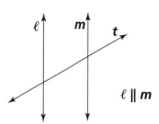

$\ell \parallel m$

Directions   Use the figure at the right for problems 1–5.

1. Name the interior angles. _____

2. Name the exterior angles. _____

3. Name eight pairs of supplementary angles.

   _____

4. Name all pairs of corresponding angles.

   _____

5. Name all pairs of alternate interior angles.

   _____

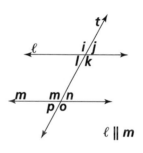

$\ell \parallel m$

Directions   Use the figure shown for problems 6–10. Name the angles as *exterior, interior,*
alternate exterior, alternate interior, corresponding, or *supplementary.*

6. $\angle a$ and $\angle e$

   _____

7. $\angle b$ and $\angle h$

   _____

8. $\angle d$ and $\angle f$

   _____

9. $\angle a$ and $\angle d$, and $\angle g$ and $\angle f$

   _____

10. $\angle c$ and $\angle b$, and $\angle e$ and $\angle h$

   _____

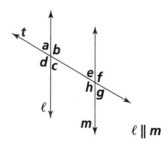

$\ell \parallel m$

Theorems Using Parallel Lines

EXAMPLE   **Theorem 3.3.1:** If two lines are parallel, then the interior angles on the same side of the transversal are supplementary.

Theorem 3.3.2: If two lines are parallel, then the corresponding angles are equal.

Theorem 3.3.3: If two lines are parallel, then the alternate interior angles are equal.

Directions   Complete the following statements.

Use the figure shown and Theorem 3.3.1 for problems 1–2.

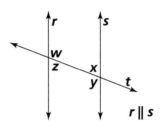

1. $m\angle y + m\angle z =$ _____

2. $m\angle x + m\angle w =$ _____

Use the same figure and Theorem 3.3.3 for problems 3–4.

3. $m\angle w =$ _____

4. $m\angle x =$ _____

Use the figure below and Theorem 3.3.2 for problems 5–10.

5. $m\angle y =$ _____

6. $m\angle w =$ _____

7. $m\angle t =$ _____

8. $m\angle z =$ _____

9. $m\angle s =$ _____

10. $m\angle u =$ _____

$\ell \parallel m$

Solving Problems with Theorems and Parallel Lines

EXAMPLE With the three theorems, you can find the measures of all eight angles with
the measure of just one.

Since ∠w is a corresponding angle to ∠s, and ∠u is a vertical
angle to ∠s, they are both equal to ∠s and measure 60°.
∠t and ∠v are both supplementary to ∠s and therefore
measure 120°.
∠y is a vertical angle to ∠w. Therefore, it also measures 60°.
∠x and ∠z are both supplementary to ∠w and therefore measure 120°.

ℓ ∥ m

Directions Find the measures of the angles in the figure. Write your reason for each
measure. Use the three theorems about parallel lines and what you know
about supplementary and vertical angles.

1. m∠b = _____

2. m∠a = _____

3. m∠c = _____

4. m∠d = _____

5. m∠e = _____

6. m∠f = _____

7. m∠g = _____

8. m∠h = _____

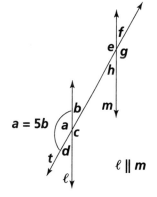

a = 5b

ℓ ∥ m

Directions Solve for x in the following problems.

9. _____

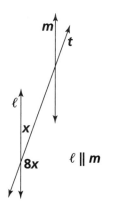

ℓ ∥ m

10. _____

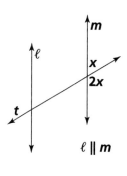

ℓ ∥ m

Constructions

EXAMPLE

Given: line *a* and point *X*   •*X*

Step 1   Draw a transversal *t* through point *X*.

Step 2   Copy ∠*s* at point *X*. This will produce alternate interior angles that are equal.

Directions   For each problem, construct a pair of parallel lines with a set of alternate interior angles that measure *x* degrees. **Hint:** Create the stated angle with one line parallel to the bottom of the page. Place point *X* on the other line and then copy the first angle.

1. $x = 60°$

2. $x = 20°$

3. $x = 100°$

4. $x = 150°$

5. $x = 90°$

6. $x = 75°$

7. $x = 175°$

8. $x = 89°$

9. $x = 5°$

10. $x = 35°$

Quadrilaterals and Parallels

EXAMPLE   A parallelogram is a quadrilateral whose opposite sides are parallel.

A rectangle is a parallelogram with four right angles.

A rhombus is a parallelogram with four equal sides.

A square is a rectangle with sides of equal length.

Directions   Use the figure at the right and the definitions and theorems about parallels to complete the following statements.

1. $\overline{AB}$ is parallel to _____.

2. $\overline{AD}$ is parallel to _____.

3. $\overline{AB}$ is not parallel to _____ and _____.

4. $\overline{AD}$ is not parallel to _____ and _____.

5. $m\angle 1 + m\angle 2 =$ _____

6. $m\angle 1 + m\angle 4 =$ _____

7. $m\angle 2 + m\angle 3 =$ _____

8. $m\angle 1 + m\angle 2 + m\angle 3 + m\angle 4 =$ _____

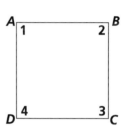

Given: ABCD is a square.

Directions   Use the figure at the right and the definitions and theorems about parallels to complete the following statements.

9. $\overline{DE}$ is parallel to _____.

10. $\overline{EF}$ is parallel to _____.

11. $m\angle 2 =$ _____

12. $m\angle 1 + m\angle 2 =$ _____

13. $m\angle 1 + m\angle 4 =$ _____

14. $m\angle 1 + m\angle 2 = m\angle 1 + m\angle 4.\ m\angle 2 =$ _____.

15. $m\angle 1 + m\angle 2 + m\angle 3 + m\angle 4 =$ _____

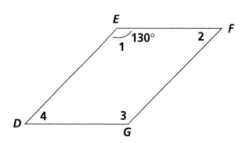

Given: DEFG is a parallelogram.

Trapezoids

| EXAMPLE | A trapezoid is a quadrilateral with exactly one pair of parallel sides.
An isosceles trapezoid is a trapezoid with two equal sides.
A right trapezoid is a trapezoid with two right angles. |

Directions Use the figure at the right to find the answers.

1. Which sides are parallel? _____

2. m∠1 = _____

3. m∠1 + m∠4 = _____

4. m∠2 + m∠3 = _____

5. Angle sum = _____

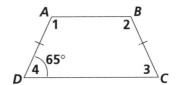

Given: ABCD is an
isosceles trapezoid.

Directions Use the figure at the right to find the answers.

6. Which sides are parallel? _____

7. m∠1 = _____

8. m∠1 + m∠4 = _____

9. m∠2 + m∠3 = _____

10. Angle sum = _____

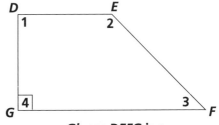

Given: DEFG is a
right trapezoid.

Directions Use the figure at the right to find the answers.

11. Which sides are parallel? _____

12. m∠2 = _____

13. m∠1 + m∠2 = _____

14. m∠3 + m∠4 = _____

15. Angle sum = _____

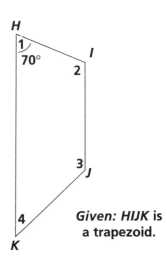

Given: HIJK is
a trapezoid.

Proving Lines Parallel

EXAMPLE	Alternate Interior Angles Postulate	If a transversal intersects two lines so that the alternate interior angles are equal, then the two lines are parallel.
	Theorem 3.7.1	If corresponding angles are equal, then the lines are parallel.

Directions   Construct parallel lines as described in problem 1 on another sheet of paper. Then answer the questions.

1. Given line *a* and a point *C* not on *a*, construct line *b* parallel to *a* through point *C*, using the Alternate Interior Angles Postulate.

   • *C*

2. Which equal angles did you use to construct line *b*? (Mark them on your construction.)

   ⟵―――――――――――――⟶ *a*

3. How could you prove these lines are parallel using the theorem above?

   _____

   _____

Directions   Construct parallel lines as described in problem 4 on another sheet of paper. Then answer the questions.

4. Given line *d* and a point *F* not on *d*, construct line *e* parallel to *d* through point *F* using the theorem above.

   • *F*

5. Which equal angles did you use to construct line *e*? (Mark them on your construction.)

   ⟵―――――――――――――⟶ *d*

6. How could you prove these lines are parallel using the Alternate Interior Angle Postulate?

   _____

   _____

More Theorems and Converses

EXAMPLE	

Converse 1 If alternate interior angles are equal, then the lines are parallel. (Alternate Interior Angles Postulate)

Converse 2 If corresponding angles are equal, then the lines are parallel. (Theorem 3.7.1)

Converse 3 If the sum of the interior angles on the same side of the transversal is 180°, then the lines are parallel. (Theorem 3.8.1)

Directions Use the diagram shown. Tell which converse you can use to prove that line x is parallel with line y if the angles have the given values.

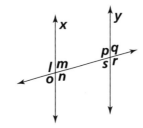

1. $m\angle q = m\angle m$ _____

2. $m\angle p = m\angle n$ _____

3. $m\angle m + m\angle p = 180°$ _____

4. $m\angle r = m\angle n$ _____

5. $m\angle l = m\angle p$ _____

6. $m\angle n + m\angle s = 180°$ _____

7. $m\angle s = m\angle o$ _____

8. $m\angle m = m\angle s$ _____

9. $m\angle s = 75°, m\angle n = 105°$ _____

10. $m\angle l = 35°, m\angle p = 35°$ _____

Algebra Connection: Solving Linear Equations

EXAMPLE   Solve $4x + 3 = 15$ for x.

Step 1 Isolate the variable term. $4x + 3 - 3 = 15 - 3$

$4x = 12$

Step 2 Divide by the constant coefficient. $\frac{4x}{4} = \frac{12}{4}$

$x = 3$

Step 3 Check. $4 \cdot (3) + 3 = 15$

Directions   Solve for each variable. Check your answers.

1. $4z = 24$ _____

2. $\frac{1}{5}e = -7$ _____

3. $n + 17 = 17$ _____

4. $-2 + p = 4$ _____

5. $6y + 19 = 1$ _____

6. $\frac{1}{2}n + 19 = 12$ _____

7. $\frac{2}{3}c + 5 = 17$ _____

8. $\frac{1}{4}x + 9 = 13$ _____

9. $\frac{4}{5}a - 7 = 9$ _____

10. $12r - 7 = 29$ _____

EXAMPLE   Of the rooms in a motel, $\frac{3}{8}$ are reserved. If nine rooms are reserved, then how many rooms are in the motel?

Step 1 Let x = number of rooms in the motel. $\frac{3}{8}x = 9$

Step 2 Solve $\frac{3}{8}x = 9$. $\frac{8}{3} \cdot \frac{3}{8}x = \frac{8}{3} \cdot 9$ $\frac{24}{24}x = \frac{72}{3}$ $x = 24$

Step 3 Check. Is $\frac{3}{8} \cdot (24) = 9$ true? $\frac{3}{8} \cdot (24) = \frac{72}{8} = 9$.   Yes, this is true.

Directions   Write an equation for each problem.
Solve it and check your answer.

11. Of the guests at a party, $\frac{4}{5}$ want water with dinner. If 16 people want water with dinner, then how many people are at the party? _____

12. If you add five to seven times some number, you get 54. What is the number? _____

13. Hue is four years younger than his sister Kim. Hue is 12. How old is Kim? _____

14. Of the students in a class, $\frac{3}{5}$ play musical instruments. If 12 students play musical instruments, then how many students are in the class? _____

15. Elvira cooked 45 hamburgers for a party. Each person ate two hamburgers. There were nine hamburgers left. How many people were at the party? _____

Graphing Ordered Pairs

EXAMPLE Graph and label this point on the coordinate plane.
Point *X* (4, –2)

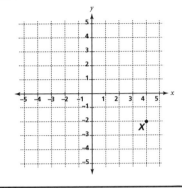

Directions Graph and label these points on the coordinate plane.

1. *A* (0, 4)

2. *B* (3, –1)

3. *C* (5, 2)

4. *D* (–3, 4)

5. *E* (–4, –1)

6. *F* (4, –5)

7. *G* (–1, –4)

8. *H* (2, –4)

9. *I* (3, 0)

10. *J* (0, 5)

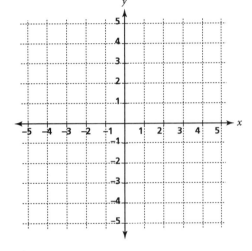

11. *K* (5, 5)

12. *L* (–5, 1)

13. *M* (5, 0)

14. *N* (3, 3)

15. *O* (–2, –2)

16. *P* (–4, 4)

17. *Q* (1, –5)

18. *R* (0, 0)

19. *S* (2, –2)

20. *T* (1, 1)

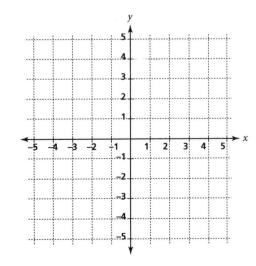

Using Formulas to Graph Ordered Pairs

EXAMPLE   Given the algebraic equation $y = 2x + 3$, graph the ordered pair of (x, y) when $x = 1$.

If $x = 1$, then $y = 2(1) + 3 = 2 + 3 = 5$.
So the ordered pair is (1, 5).

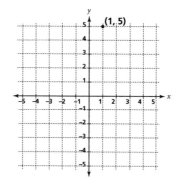

Directions   Use the following equations to find the x- or y-value that is not given. Graph the ordered pairs on the coordinate plane below.

$y = x - 2$

1. $x = 3$ _____

2. $x = 5$ _____

3. $y = 0$ _____

4. $x = -3$ _____

5. $y = -4$ _____

$y = 3x$

6. $x = 2$ _____

7. $y = 3$ _____

8. $x = -3$ _____

9. $y = -6$ _____

10. $x = 0$ _____

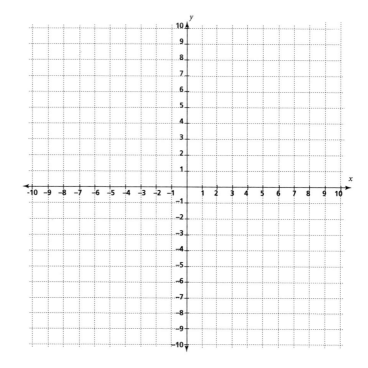

Graphing Horizontal Lines

EXAMPLE   Graph this line.

$y = 2$ and x is any real number

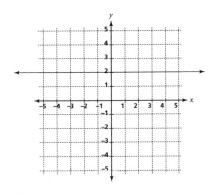

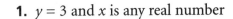

Directions   Draw a graph of each line and label it.

1. $y = 3$ and x is any real number

2. $y = -1$ and x is any real number

3. $y = 4$ and x is any real number

4. $y = -2$ and x is any real number

5. $y = -5$ and x is any real number

6. $y = 0$ and x is any real number

7. $y = 2$ and x is any real number

8. $y = -3$ and x is any real number

9. $y = 5$ and x is any real number

10. $y = -4$ and x is any real number

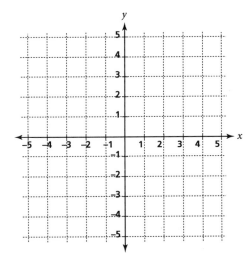

Graphing Ordered Pairs (Horizontal Lines)

EXAMPLE	Draw a graph of this line and label it.

(*x*, 3) where *x* is any real number

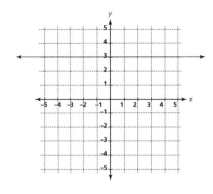

Directions   Draw a graph of each line and label it.

1. (*x*, –3) where *x* is any real number

2. (*x*, 1) where *x* is any real number

3. (*x*, –2) where *x* is any real number

4. (*x*, 5) where *x* is any real number

5. (*x*, –4) where *x* is any real number

6. (*x*, 0) where *x* is any real number

7. (*x*, –5) where *x* is any real number

8. (*x*, 2) where *x* is any real number

9. (*x*, 4) where *x* is any real number

10. (*x*, –1) where *x* is any real number

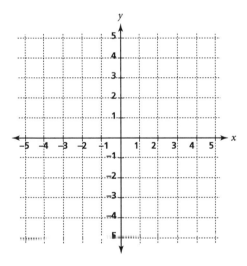

Graphing Vertical Lines

EXAMPLE   Draw a graph of this line and label it.

$x = 1$ and y is any real number

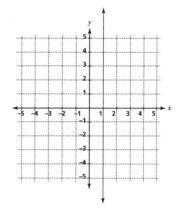

Directions   Draw a graph of each line and label it.

1. $x = -2$ and y is any real number

2. $x = -1$ and y is any real number

3. $x = 3$ and y is any real number

4. $x = -4$ and y is any real number

5. $x = 5$ and y is any real number

6. $x = 0$ and y is any real number

7. $x = 2$ and y is any real number

8. $x = -5$ and y is any real number

9. $x = -3$ and y is any real number

10. $x = 4$ and y is any real number

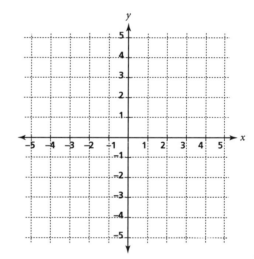

Graphing Ordered Pairs (Vertical Lines)

EXAMPLE   Draw a graph of this line and label it.

(–4, y) where y is any real number

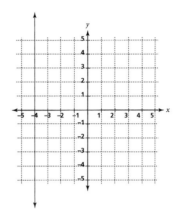

Directions   Draw a graph of each line and label it.

1. (4, y) where y is any real number

2. (1, y) where y is any real number

3. (2, y) where y is any real number

4. (–5, y) where y is any real number

5. (3, y) where y is any real number

6. (0, y) where y is any real number

7. (–2, y) where y is any real number

8. (–1, y) where y is any real number

9. (5, y) where y is any real number

10. (–3, y) where y is any real number

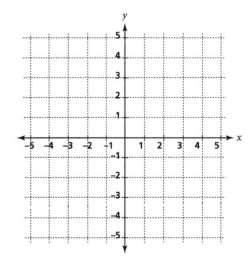

Finding the Slope of a Line

EXAMPLE   Find the slope, *m,* of a line that passes through these points.

(0, 0) and (6, 3)

The formula for finding the slope of a line is $\frac{y_1 - y_2}{x_1 - x_2} = m$.

Put the given points into the formula: $\frac{0-3}{0-6} = \frac{-3}{-6} = \frac{1}{2}$.

The slope is $\frac{1}{2}$.

Directions   Find the slope of the line that passes through the given points.

1. (−2, 5) and (4, 0)   _____

2. (0, 3) and (−2, 4)   _____

3. (−3, 4) and (−5, 6)   _____

4. (3, −2) and (4, 0)   _____

5. (5, 5) and (3, 1)   _____

6. (−2, −1) and (−3, 1)   _____

7. (−4, −3) and (4, 1)   _____

8. (2, −1) and (2, 5)   _____

9. (0, 2) and (1, 7)   _____

10. (3, 3) and (−3, 0)   _____

11. (0, 0) and (3, 3)   _____

12. (−4, 2) and (4, 2)   _____

13. (−3, 5) and (−2, 0)   _____

14. (2, 2) and (−3, −3)   _____

15. (−4, 3) and (−5, 6)   _____

The Slope of Parallel Lines

Find the slope for this pair of lines.

The formula for finding the slope of a line is $\frac{y_1 - y_2}{x_1 - x_2} = m$.

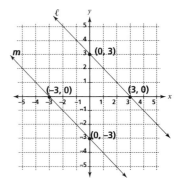

Put the given points into the formula:

line ℓ $\frac{0-3}{3-0} = \frac{-3}{3} = -1$

line m $\frac{0-(-3)}{-3-0} = \frac{3}{-3} = -1$

The slope formula shows that both line ℓ and line m have a slope of -1.

Directions   Find the slope for each pair of lines.

1. _____

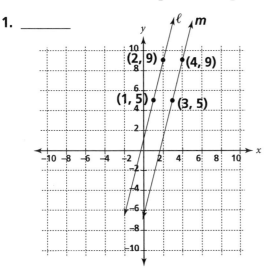

2. _____

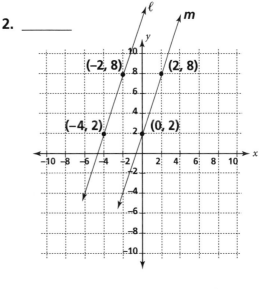

3. _____

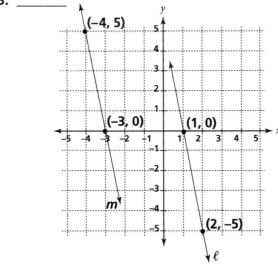

4. _____

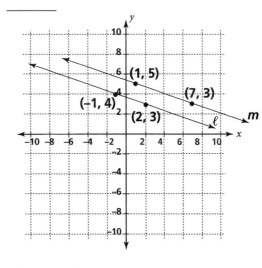

y = mx + b

EXAMPLE

Write the equation of line ℓ. Use the form $y = mx + b$.

The slope formula shows that $\frac{y_1 - y_2}{x_1 - x_2} = \frac{4-2}{4-3} = \frac{2}{1} = 2 = m$.

To solve for b, put one point's x- and y-values plus the value for m into the formula $y = mx + b$.

Using the first point, $2 = 2(3) + b$; $2 = 6 + b$; $b = -4$.

The equation is written as $y = 2x - 4$.

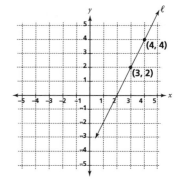

Directions Write the equation of line ℓ. Use the form $y = mx + b$.

1. _____

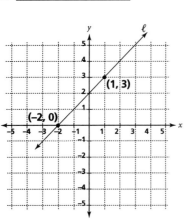

2. _____

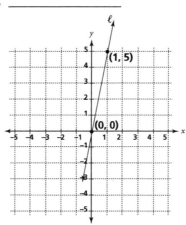

3. _____

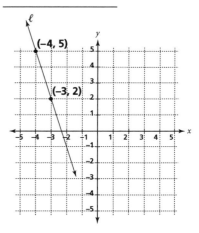

4. _____

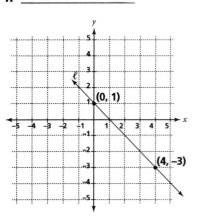

5. _____

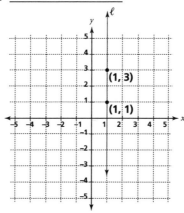

Using Slope in Real-Life Examples

EXAMPLE A staircase has 10 stairs that are 8 inches high and 12 inches deep. If the base of the staircase is at (0, 0), what are the staircase's domain, range, and slope? What would the ordered pair for the top of the staircase be if the numbers were counted in inches?

The domain of the staircase is 108 inches. Because the depth of the last stair is actually part of the second floor, the domain is the depth of each stair, or 12 times the nine stairs that have depth, giving 108 inches.

The range of the staircase is 80 inches—the number of stairs (10) times the height of each stair (8).

The slope of the staircase is $\frac{2}{3}$.

The ordered pair for the top of the staircase is (108, 80).

Directions Solve the following problems.

A surveyor finds that a nearby hill's crest has a horizontal distance of 300 feet from the spot where she is standing. The elevation of the hill's crest is 100 feet.

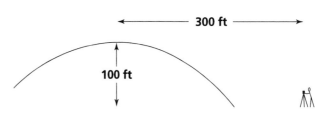

1. What are the domain, range, and slope of the hill from where she is standing to the crest? _____

A diagonal is drawn from opposite corners of a rectangle. The rectangle is standing on one of its shorter sides, which is 4 inches, and the slope of the diagonal is 2.

2. What is the length of the two longer sides? _____

3. What are the domain and range of the diagonal? _____

A seesaw has a horizontal distance of 10 feet from one seat to the other. The vertical distance of the seat not resting on the ground is 4 feet.

4. What are the domain, range, and slope of the seesaw? _____

5. Write an equation for each problem.

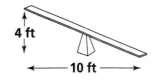

hill _____

diagonal _____

seesaw _____

Writing the Equation of a Line

EXAMPLE   Graph this line using the slope
and point given.

Line ℓ; $m = 2$, passes through (3, 4)

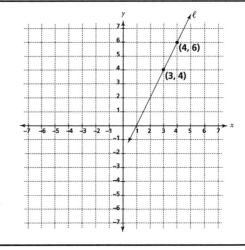

Directions   Graph each line using the slope
and point given. Label each line.

1. Line a; $m = \frac{1}{2}$, passes through (2, –1)

2. Line b; $m = -2$, passes through (0, –3)

3. Line c; $m = -\frac{3}{4}$, passes through (3, 5)

4. Line d; $m = 3$, passes through (–5, 1)

5. Line e; $m = \frac{5}{2}$, passes through (2, 0)

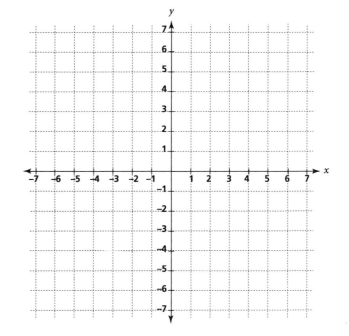

Directions   Write the equation for each line
you graphed in problems 1–5.

6. Line a _____

7. Line b _____

8. Line c _____

9. Line d _____

10. Line e _____

Name _____ Date _____ Period _____

More Equations

EXAMPLE Graph this line using the slope
and point given.

Line ℓ; $m = -\frac{1}{6}$, passes through (–2, 5)

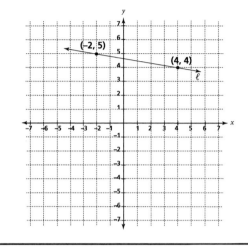

Directions Graph each line using the slope
and point given. Label each line.

1. Line a; $m = -\frac{5}{4}$, passes through (–3, –2)

2. Line b; $m = 3$, passes through (0, 0)

3. Line c; $m = -4$, passes through (–5, 5)

4. Line d; $m = \frac{3}{7}$, passes through (–2, –4)

5. Line e; $m = -\frac{3}{2}$, passes through (1, 1)

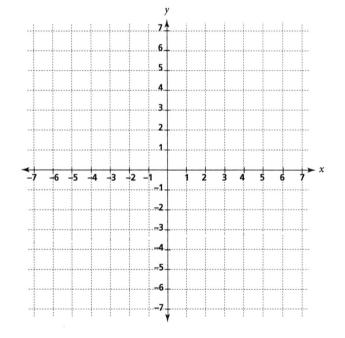

Directions Write the equation for each line
you graphed in problems 1–5.

6. Line a _____

7. Line b _____

8. Line c _____

9. Line d _____

10. Line e _____

The Midpoint of a Segment

EXAMPLE   Review the midpoint formula.

$\frac{x_1 + x_2}{2}$ = midpoint *x*-value

$\frac{y_1 + y_2}{2}$ = midpoint *y*-value

$\frac{6 + 0}{2} = \frac{6}{2} = 3$ = midpoint *x*-value

$\frac{4 + 0}{2} = \frac{4}{2} = 2$ = midpoint *y*-value

The midpoint of the line segment is (3, 2).

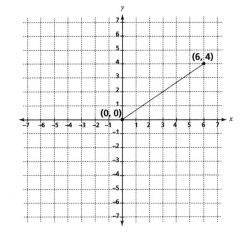

Directions   Find the midpoints of the following line segments.
Be sure to give both coordinates of each midpoint.

1. _____

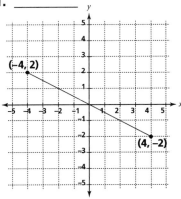

2. _____

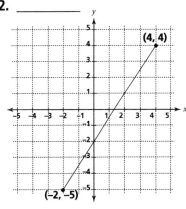

3. _____

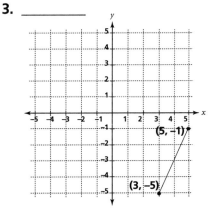

4. _____

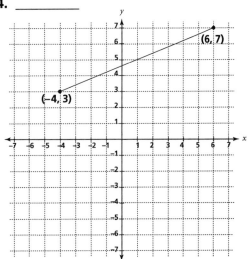

5. _____

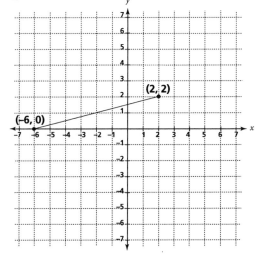

Graphing Line Segments

EXAMPLE   Use the point and the midpoint given to find the other endpoint
of the line segment.

(0, 0) is the first endpoint of the line segment.

(3, 3) is the midpoint of the line segment.

Using the midpoint formula, you can solve for the line segment's
other endpoint.

(x_1, y_1) = (0, 0), midpoint x-value = 3, midpoint y-value = 3

$\frac{0 + x_2}{2}$ = 3; $\frac{x_2}{2}$ = 3; multiply each side by 2; x_2 = 6

$\frac{0 + y_2}{2}$ = 3; $\frac{y_2}{2}$ = 3; multiply each side by 2; y_2 = 6

The other endpoint is at (6, 6).

Directions   Find the second endpoint for each line segment using the given endpoint
and midpoint. Then graph and label the line segment with both endpoints
and midpoint on a coordinate plane.

1. Endpoint = (4, 6);
midpoint = (2, 0)   _____

2. Endpoint = (−3, −5);
midpoint = (−1, −1)   _____

3. Endpoint = (5, 4);
midpoint = (3, 1)   _____

4. Endpoint = (3, −5);
midpoint = (−1, −2)   _____

5. Endpoint = (−2, 6);
midpoint = (1, 1)   _____

6. Endpoint = (−5, −3);
midpoint = (−4, −2)   _____

7. Endpoint = (4, 4);
midpoint = (5, −2)   _____

8. Endpoint = (1, 7);
midpoint = (3, 2)   _____

9. Endpoint = (−3, −4);
midpoint = (1, −1)   _____

10. Endpoint = (1, 1);
midpoint = (2, 0)   _____

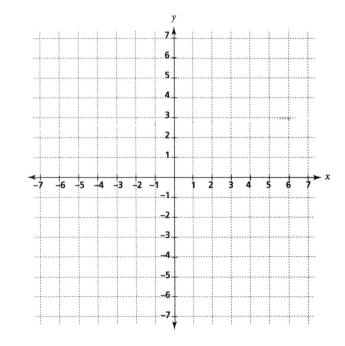

Algebra Connection: Rate and Mixture Problems

EXAMPLE   Monya drove at 60 mph for 2 h and then at 30 mph for 3 h.
What was her average rate of speed?

$d = rt$ $d = (60 \cdot 2) + (30 \cdot 3) = 120 + 90 = 210$ $t = 2 + 3 = 5$

$r = \frac{d}{t} = \frac{210}{5} = 42$ Her average rate of speed was 42 mph.

Directions   Solve.

1. Ken biked at an average rate of 12 mph for 2 h. How many miles did he go?   _____

2. Pat traveled 280 mi in 7 h. What was her average rate of speed?   _____

3. Hue drove at 55 mph for 2 h and then at 45 mph for 3 h.
   What was his average rate of speed?   _____

4. Joe drove at 80 kph for $2\frac{1}{2}$ h and then at 120 kph for $1\frac{1}{2}$ h.
   What was his average rate of speed?   _____

EXAMPLE   Juice costs $3.00 per gallon. Soda costs $1.50 per gallon. You mix 4 gallons
of juice and 2 gallons of soda. How much does 1 gallon of this mixture cost?

You pay ($3.00 • 4) + ($1.50 • 2) = $15.00. You make 4 + 2 = 6 gallons.
The cost is $15.00 ÷ 6 = $2.50 for 1 gallon.

Directions   Solve.

5. Juice A costs $6.00 per gallon. Juice B costs $3.00 per gallon.
   You mix 4 gallons of juice A and 2 gallons of juice B to make
   punch. How much does 1 gallon of this punch cost?   _____

6. Walnuts cost $4.50 per pound. Almonds cost $6.00 per pound.
   You mix 3 pounds of walnuts and 3 pounds of almonds.
   How much should 1 pound of this mixture cost?   _____

7. Peanuts cost $2.50 per pound. Filberts cost $5.50 per pound.
   You mix $1\frac{1}{2}$ pounds of peanuts and $\frac{1}{2}$ pound of filberts.
   How much should 1 pound of this mixture cost?   _____

8. Juice A costs $3.50 per gallon. Soda costs $1.10 per gallon.
   You mix $3\frac{1}{2}$ gallons of juice A and $1\frac{1}{2}$ gallons of soda to
   make punch. How much does 1 gallon of this punch cost?   _____

Triangle Sides

EXAMPLE Equilateral triangles have three equal sides.

Isosceles triangles have two equal sides.

Scalene triangles have no equal sides.

Is a triangle with the following side lengths an equilateral, isosceles, or scalene triangle?

Q. Triangle *ABC* has sides that measure 8, 9, and 9 units.

A. Triangle *ABC* is an isosceles triangle.

Directions Identify each triangle as *equilateral, isosceles,* or *scalene.*

1. Triangle *ABC* has sides that measure 3, 3, and 3 units in length. _____

2. Triangle *EFG* has sides that measure 9, 17, and 14 units in length. _____

3. Triangle *HIJ* has sides that measure 4, 4, and 7 units in length. _____

4. Triangle *KLM* has sides that measure 8, 10, and 8 units in length. _____

5. Triangle *NOP* has sides that measure 8, 9, and 11 units in length. _____

6. Triangle *QRS* has sides that measure 8, 8, and 8 units in length. _____

7. Triangle *TUV* has sides that measure 2, 3, and 4 units in length. _____

8. Triangle *WXY* has sides that measure 19, 19, and 30 units in length. _____

9. Triangle *DZA* has sides that measure 7.5, 7.5, and 7.5 units in length. _____

10. Triangle *BTU* has sides that measure 6, 7, and 10 units in length. _____

11. Line segment *AB* in triangle *ABC* is equal to line segment *AC* and four times the length of line segment *BC*. _____

12. Line segment *DE* in triangle *DEF* is equal to line segment *EF* and line segment *DF*. _____

13. Line segment *XY* in triangle *XYZ* is not equal to either line segment *YZ* or *XZ*. _____

14. Line segment *WX* in triangle *WXY* is equal to line segment *XY* and not congruent to line segment *YW*. _____

15. Line segment *XY* in triangle *XYZ* is equal to line segments *YZ* and *XZ*. _____

Naming Triangles by Their Angles

EXAMPLE   Acute triangles have three angles less than 90°.

Obtuse triangles have one obtuse angle greater than 90°.

Right triangles have one 90° angle.

Equilateral triangles have three equal angles.

Isosceles triangles have two equal angles.

Scalene triangles have no equal angles.

Directions   Name each of these triangles using its angles.

1. Triangle *ABC* has angles that measure 100°, 40°, and 40°. _____

2. Triangle *DEF* has angles that measure 60°, 70°, and 50°. _____

3. Triangle *GHI* has angles that measure 60°, 60°, and 60°. _____

4. Triangle *JKL* has angles that measure 110°, 30°, and 40°. _____

5. Triangle *MNO* has angles that measure 90°, 45°, and 45°. _____

6. Triangle *PQR* has angles that measure 90°, 40°, and 50°. _____

7. Triangle *STU* has angles that measure 80°, 50°, and 50°. _____

8. Triangle *VWX* has angles that measure 130°, 30°, and 20°. _____

9. ∠*BAC* in triangle *ABC* measures 60° and is equal to ∠*ABC*. _____

10. ∠*BAC* in triangle *ABC* measures 90°, and ∠*ABC* and ∠*BCA* are not equal to each other. _____

Constructing Triangles Using Their Angles

EXAMPLE   Construct △ABC with 2m∠CAB = m∠ACB
and m∠B = 90°.

Step 1 Draw a right angle. Label it ∠B.

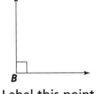

Step 2 Pick a point along one of the rays of ∠B. Label this point A.
Using your protractor, draw an angle that measures 30° using
point A as the vertex and one ray of ∠B as one side. Extend
the new ray so that it crosses the other ray of ∠B. Label the
point where it crosses, point C.

Step 3 Measure ∠ACB. It should measure 60°. You have now
constructed a right triangle with acute angles that have a ratio
of 2 to 1. This triangle is a type of right scalene triangle.

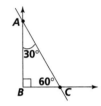

Directions   Complete the following constructions. Use a separate sheet
of paper. You will need a straightedge and a protractor.

1. Construct an isosceles triangle in which the sum of its two
   equal angles equals the measure of its third angle.

2. Construct an isosceles triangle in which the sum of its two
   equal angles is equal to $\frac{1}{2}$ the measure of its third angle.

3. Construct a scalene triangle that has a right angle and two
   other angles with a ratio of 8 to 1.

4. Construct an equilateral triangle by drawing one 60° angle
   and then another 60° angle off one of the first angle's rays.

5. Construct an isosceles triangle in which the sum of its two
   equal angles is equal to twice the measure of its third angle.

Special Quadrilaterals

EXAMPLE   Identify whether a quadrilateral with the following parameters is possible.

Figure *ABCD* has four sides. Side $\overline{AB}$ is equal to side $\overline{CD}$. ∠*DAB* and ∠*DCB* are right angles.

Solution: Figure *ABCD* is either a square or a rectangle.

Directions   Is a quadrilateral with the following parameters possible? Write *True* if it can exist or *False* if it cannot exist. If the figure can exist, identify which type of quadrilateral the figure is.

1. Figure *ABCD* has four sides that are equal. Two of its angles each measure 70° and the other two angles each measure 110°.   _____

2. Figure *ABCD* has four sides. $\overline{CD}$ is twice the length of $\overline{AB}$. ∠*ADC* and ∠*DCB* both measure 60°.   _____

3. Figure *ABCD* has four sides that are equal. Three of its angles each measure 85° and the fourth angle measures 95°.   _____

4. Figure *ABCD* has four sides that are not equal. The measures of its angles are 88°, 89°, 91°, and 92°.   _____

5. Figure *ABCD* has four sides. Three of these sides are of equal length. The fourth side is twice the length of any of the other sides. The figure also has two sets of equal angles.   _____

6. Figure *ABCD* has four sides. These sides are two pairs of equal lengths, neither of which is equal to the other pair's length. The figure also has two pairs of equal angles, neither of which is equal to the other pair's measure.   _____

7. Figure *ABCD* has four sides. Two of these sides are parallel. Two of the figure's angles are right angles. The other two angles are not right angles.   _____

8. Figure *ABCD* has four sides. The figure has two pairs of equal sides, neither of which is equal to the other. The figure has two equal angles and one angle that is larger than 180°.   _____

9. Figure *ABCD* has four sides that are equal. The figure's angles measure 87°, 87°, 93°, and 91°.   _____

10. Figure *ABCD* has four sides that are not equal. The figure has four angles that are equal.   _____

Diagonals

EXAMPLE Review the following proof.

Given: *ABCD* is a square, $\overline{AC}$ is a diagonal, and m∠1 = 45°.

Problem: Find the measures of ∠2, ∠3, and ∠4.

Statement	Reason
1. m∠1 = 45°	1. Given.
2. ∠*A* is a right angle.	2. Given: definition of a square.
3. m∠1 + m∠2 = 90° and 45° + m∠2 = 90°	3. Substitution of equals.
4. m∠2 = 45°	4. Subtraction of equals.
5. $\overline{BC}$ is parallel to $\overline{AD}$ and $\overline{AC}$ is a transversal.	5. Given: definition of a square and transversal.
6. Therefore, m∠4 = m∠2 = 45°	6. Alternate interior angles.
7. $\overline{AB}$ is parallel to $\overline{DC}$ and $\overline{AC}$ is a transversal.	7. Given: definition of a square and transversal.
8. Therefore, m∠1 = m∠3 = 45°	8. Alternate interior angles.

You have proven that angles 1, 2, 3, and 4 each measure 45°.

Directions Complete the problems. Write the missing reasons.

Given: *WXYZ* is a rectangle, $\overline{WY}$ is a diagonal.
Problem: Show that ∠1 ≅ ∠3 and ∠2 ≅ ∠4.

1. $\overline{XY}$ is parallel to $\overline{WZ}$.
1. _____

2. m∠1 = m∠3
2. _____

3. $\overline{WX}$ is parallel to $\overline{ZY}$.
3. _____

4. m∠2 = m∠4
4. _____

Given: for the above rectangle *WXYZ*, ∠1 is five times the measure of ∠2.
Problem: Find the measures of ∠1 and ∠2.

5. ∠*W* is a right angle.
5. _____

6. m∠1 + m∠2 = 90°
6. _____

7. m∠2 = 15°
7. _____

8. m∠1 = 75°
8. _____

Given: *WXYZ* is a parallelogram with diagonal $\overline{WY}$.
Problem: Show that ∠1 ≅ ∠3.

9. $\overline{XY}$ is parallel to $\overline{WZ}$.
9. _____

10. m∠1 = m∠3
10. _____

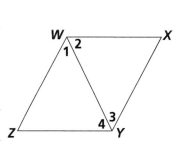

More Diagonals

EXAMPLE

Given: WXYZ is a rectangle with diagonal $\overline{WY}$ and m∠1 is four times as large as m∠2.

Problem: Find the measures of ∠1, ∠2, ∠3, and ∠4.

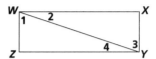

Solution

∠W is a right angle. m∠1 + m∠2 = 90°

Find m∠1 and m∠2.   4m∠2 + m∠2 = 90°   5m∠2 = 90°   m∠2 = 18°

   m∠2 = 18°   m∠1 = 4m∠2 = 72°

   m∠1 = 72°

Find m∠3 and m∠4.

   m∠1 = m∠3   alternate interior angles

   m∠2 = m∠4   alternate interior angles

m∠1 and m∠3 = 72° and m∠2 and m∠4 = 18°

Directions Find the measures of the angles.

Given: EFGH is a rectangle with diagonal $\overline{EG}$ and ∠3 is eight times as large as ∠4.

1. m∠1 = _____

2. m∠2 = _____

3. m∠3 = _____

4. m∠4 = _____

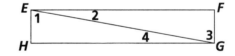

Given: JKLM is a rectangle with diagonal $\overline{JL}$ and ∠1 is twice as large as ∠2.

5. m∠1 = _____

6. m∠2 = _____

7. m∠3 = _____

8. m∠4 = _____

Given: MNOP is a rectangle with diagonal $\overline{MO}$ and ∠3 is seventeen times as large as ∠4.

9. m∠1 = _____

10. m∠2 = _____

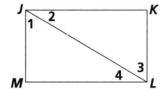

Triangle Angles

EXAMPLE   Find the measure of ∠x.

The angle sum of any triangle is 180°.

You are given the measures of two angles (the 90° right angle and the 55° angle) and are asked to find the measure of the third.

You can write the equation 180° = 90° + 55° + x. This can be reduced to 180° = 145° + x. Subtract 145° from both sides to get x = 35°.

Directions   Find the measure of ∠x.

1.

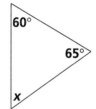

_____

2.

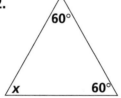

_____

3.

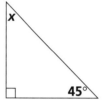

_____

4.

_____

5.

_____

6.

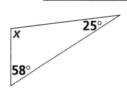

_____

7.

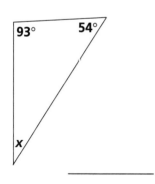

_____

8.

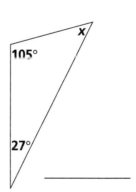

_____

9.

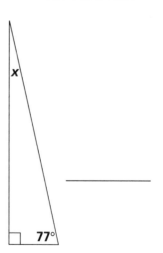

_____

10.

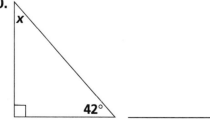

_____

Triangle Angles and Algebra

EXAMPLE   Find the value of *x*.

You know that all triangles have angle measures that total 180°.

You are given the measure of one angle and variable measures for the other two angles. You can write the equation 180° = 90° + *x* + *x*. This can be reduced to 180° = 90° + 2*x*. Subtract 90° from both sides to get 90° = 2*x*. Divide both sides by 2 to get *x* = 45°.

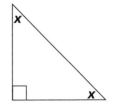

Directions   Find the value of *x*.

1.

_____

2.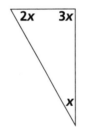

_____

3.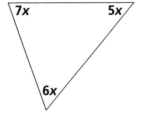

_____

4.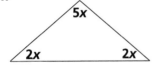

_____

5.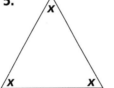

_____

6.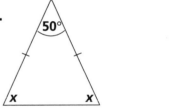

_____

7.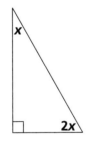

_____

8.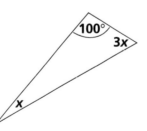

_____

9.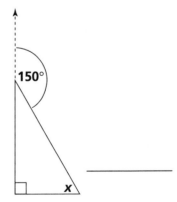

_____

10.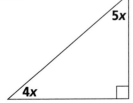

_____

Constructing Regular Polygons

EXAMPLE   Construct a regular pentagon using *XY* as the length of the sides.

Calculate the measure of the pentagon's interior angles. The degrees in a polygon can be found using the formula $(n - 2) \bullet (180°)$ where *n* is the number of sides the polygon has. Write the equation $(5 - 2) \bullet (180°)$. Calculate $3 \bullet 180° = 540°$.

A pentagon has five interior angles. Find out the measure of each angle in a regular pentagon by dividing the total number of degrees by the number of equal interior angles. $\frac{540}{5} = 108$. Each angle of a regular pentagon = 108°.

Step 1 Using a protractor, draw an angle that measures 108°. Label the vertex point *A*.

Step 2 Open your compass to match $\overline{XY}$. Using point *A* as the center of a circle, draw an arc on both rays of ∠*A*. Label the points where the arcs cross the rays, *B* and *E*.

Step 3 Copy ∠*BAE* at *B* and extend the new ray. Open the compass to match $\overline{XY}$ and draw an arc on the newest ray. Label the point where the arc crosses the ray, *C*.

Step 4 Copy ∠*BAE* at *C* and extend its new ray. Open the compass to match $\overline{XY}$ and draw an arc on this new ray. Label this point *D*. Connect *D* and *E* to complete the regular pentagon.

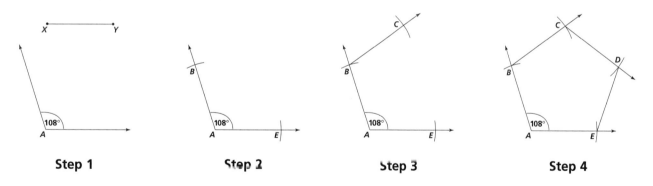

Step 1   Step 2   Step 3   Step 4

Directions Do the following constructions on a separate sheet of paper. Use a protractor to draw the first angle and then a straightedge and a compass to complete the polygon.

1. Construct a regular pentagon.

2. Construct a regular octagon.

3. Construct a regular decagon.

4. Construct a regular septagon.

5. Construct a regular hexagon.

Geometric Patterns

EXAMPLE   Use a straightedge to draw all of the possible diagonals from one vertex in this polygon.

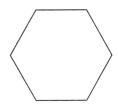 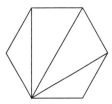

Directions   Draw all of the diagonals from one vertex in each of these polygons.

1.

2.

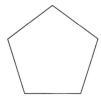

3.

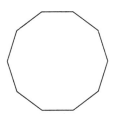

4.

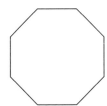

5.

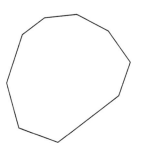

Constructing Perpendiculars

EXAMPLE   Construct a line perpendicular to line *m* that passes through point *X*.   *m*

Step 1   Open your compass to a distance somewhat greater than the distance from
              X to *m*. Using *X* as the center of a circle, draw an arc that intersects *m* in
              two places. Label the points *A* and *B*.   *X*

Step 2   Keeping your compass opening constant, and using *A* as the center of a circle,
              draw an arc above *m*. Then, with the same compass opening, draw a second arc
              above *m* using *B* as the center. Label the point where the arcs intersect, *C*.

Step 3   Connect *X* and *C*. $\overline{XC}$ is perpendicular to *m*.

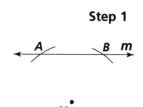

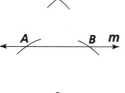
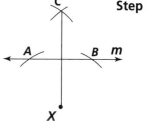

Step 1   **Step 2**   **Step 3**

Directions   Do the following constructions on a separate sheet of paper.
                Use only a compass and a straightedge.

1. Construct a ⊥ to $\overline{AB}$
    that passes through *C*.

2. Construct a ⊥ to $\overline{AB}$
    that passes through *D*.

3. Construct a ⊥ to $\overline{AB}$ that
    passes through *C*, to $\overline{BC}$
    that passes through *A*,
    and to $\overline{AC}$ that
    passes through *B*.

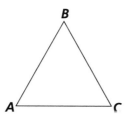
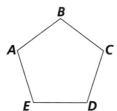
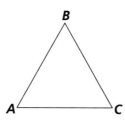

4. Construct a ⊥ to $\overline{AB}$ that
    passes through *D*, to $\overline{BC}$
    that passes through *E*, to
    $\overline{CD}$ that passes through
    A, to $\overline{DE}$ that passes
    through *B*, and to $\overline{EA}$
    that passes through *C*.

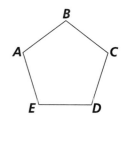

5. Draw a right triangle. Construct a ⊥ from the
    right angle to the opposite side.

More Perpendiculars

EXAMPLE   Construct a line perpendicular to *m* and through point *X*.

Step 1   Open your compass to any radius. Using *X* as the center of a circle, draw
an arc that intersects *m* in two places. Label the points *A* and *B*.

Step 2   Increase your compass opening slightly, and using *A* and then *B* as the
centers, draw intersecting arcs either above or below *m*. Label the point
where the arcs intersect, *C*.

Step 3   Draw $\overline{XC}$. $\overline{XC}$ is perpendicular to *m*.

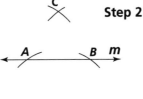

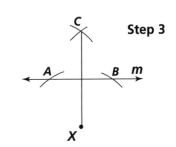

Directions   Draw perpendiculars to ℓ through all of the points shown.
Use a compass and straightedge.

1. point *A*

2. point *B*

3. point *C*

4. point *D*

5. point *E*

6. point *F*

7. point *G*

8. point *H*

9. point *I*

10. point *J*

Name _____ Date _____ Period _____

Angle Bisectors and Medians

EXAMPLE   Angle Bisectors   intersect at the in-center
Medians   intersect at the centroid

Directions   Complete the following constructions. Use a straightedge and a compass.
(Note: You may find it easier to use large triangles for your constructions.)

1. Draw any acute triangle and label it *ABC.*
   Construct its angle bisectors and label the in-center.

2. Draw any obtuse triangle and label it *EFG.*
   Construct its angle bisectors and label the in-center.

3. Draw any right triangle and label it *HIJ.*
   Construct its angle bisectors and label the in-center.

4. Draw any acute triangle and label it *KLM.*
   Construct its medians and label the centroid.

5. Draw any obtuse triangle and label it *NOP.*
   Construct its medians and label the centroid.

Altitudes

EXAMPLE   Altitudes intersect at the orthocenter.

Acute triangles have altitudes completely within the triangles.

Obtuse triangles have two exterior altitudes and one interior altitude.

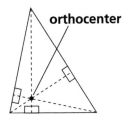

orthocenter

Directions   Complete the following constructions. Use a straightedge and a compass. (Note: You may find it easier to use large triangles for your constructions.)

1. Draw any acute triangle and label it *ABC*.
Construct its altitudes and label the orthocenter.

2. Draw any obtuse triangle and label it *ABC*.
Construct its altitudes and label the orthocenter.

3. Draw any right triangle and label it *ABC*.
Construct its altitudes and label the orthocenter.

Directions   Answer the following questions using the given information.

Given: Triangle *ABC*'s largest angle is equal to *x*.

4. Based on problems 1–3, what can you conclude about
triangle *ABC*'s orthocenter if *x* is less than 90°? _____

5. What happens to the orthocenter as *x* increases towards 90°?

_____

What happens to the orthocenter as *x* reaches 90°?

_____

What happens to the orthocenter as *x* increases to larger than 90°?

_____

Angle Sum Theorem

EXAMPLE Use the Angle Sum Theorem or its corollary to find the measures of the angles.

The topmost angle and its two adjacent angles form line ℓ, which is equivalent to a straight angle. Therefore, the sum of the topmost angle and its adjacent angles is equal to 180°. You can solve for y by writing the following equation:

$180° = y + y + y$, which can be reduced to $180° = 3y$. Divide both sides by 3 to get $y = 60°$.

The Angle Sum Theorem allows you to solve for x. The theorem states that the sum of any triangle's angles must equal 180°. You can write the following equation.

$$180° = y + x + x$$
$$180° = 60° + 2x$$
$$120° = 2x$$

$x = 60°$ You have now found the measures of all three angles in $\triangle ABC$.

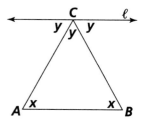

Directions Use the Angle Sum Theorem or its corollary to find the measures of the angles.

1. Angle A _____

2. Angle B _____

3. Angle C _____

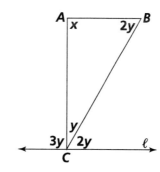

4. Angle A _____

5. Angle B _____

6. Angle C _____

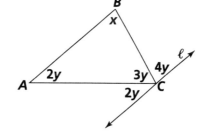

7. Angle A _____

8. Angle B _____

9. Angle C _____

10. $\angle A + \angle B + \angle C$ _____

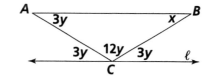

More of the Angle Sum Theorem

EXAMPLE   Use the Angle Sum Theorem or its corollary to find the measures of the angles.

The angle adjacent to $\angle C$ (labeled $2y$) is supplementary to $\angle C$ (labeled y). Therefore, the sum of $\angle C$ and the angle labeled $2y$ is $180°$. You can write the following equation to solve for y: $180° = y + 2y$. This can be reduced to $180° = 3y$. Divide both sides by 3 to get $y = 60°$.

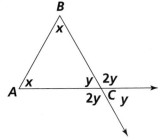

The Angle Sum Theorem allows you to solve for x. The theorem states that the sum of any triangle's angles must equal $180°$. You can write the following equations.

$$180° = y + x + x$$

$$180° = 60° + 2x$$

$$120° = 2x$$

    $x = 60°$ You have now found the measures of all three angles in $\triangle ABC$.

Directions   Use the Angle Sum Theorem or its corollary to find the measures of the angles.

1. Angle A _____

2. Angle B _____

3. Angle C _____

4. Angle A _____

5. Angle B _____

6. Angle C _____

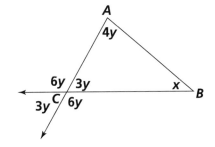

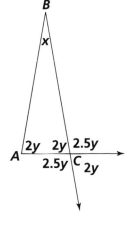

7. Angle A _____

8. Angle B _____

9. Angle C _____

10. $\angle A + \angle B + \angle C$ _____

Algebra Connection: Special Polynomial Products

EXAMPLE   Use a pattern to find the product. $(x - 4)^2$

The pattern is $(a + b)^2 = a^2 + 2ab + b^2$.

Substitute x for a and -4 for b in the pattern.

$(x - 4)^2 = x^2 + 2(x) \cdot (-4) + (-4)^2 = x^2 - 8x + 16$

Directions   Use the pattern above to find each product.

1. $(m + n)^2$ _____   **4.** $(-3 - 4d)^2$ _____

2. $(x - y)^2$ _____   **5.** $(c + 2b)^2$ _____

3. $(-5 + y)^2$ _____

EXAMPLE   Use a pattern to factor the product. $x^2 - 16$

The pattern is $(a + b)(a - b) = a^2 - b^2$.

Substitute x^2 for a^2 and 16 for b^2 in the pattern.

$x^2 - 16 = x^2 - 4^2 = (x + 4)(x - 4)$

Directions   Use the pattern above to find or factor each product.

6. $(x + 7)(x - 7)$ _____   **9.** $s^2 - 25$ _____

7. $(z + 8)(z - 8)$ _____   **10.** $p^2 - 121$ _____

8. $(-6 + y)(-6 - y)$ _____

EXAMPLE   Use a pattern to find the product. $(y + 3)^3$

The pattern is $(a + b)^3 = a^3 + 3a^2b + 3ab^2 + b^3$.

Substitute y for a and 3 for b in the pattern.

$(y + 3)^3 = (y)^3 + 3(y)^2 \cdot (3) + 3y \cdot (3)^2 + (3)^3 = y^3 + 9y^2 + 27y + 27$

Directions   Use the pattern above to find each product.

11. $(x + y)^3$ _____   **14.** $(z - 6)^3$ _____

12. $(y + 4)^3$ _____   **15.** $(c - 2)^3$ _____

13. $(a - b)^3$ _____

Proving Triangles Congruent by SAS

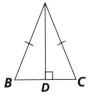

EXAMPLE   Use the SAS theorem to prove that $\triangle ABD$ and $\triangle ACD$ are congruent.

Given: $\triangle ABC$ is an isosceles triangle with $AB = AC$.

$\overline{AD}$ is the median and altitude of vertex A.

To Prove: $\triangle ABD$ and $\triangle ACD$ are congruent.

Statement	Reason
1. Point D is the midpoint of $\overline{BC}$.	1. Definition of a median.
2. $BD = CD$	2. Definition of a midpoint.
3. $m\angle BDA = 90°$	3. Definition of an altitude.
4. $m\angle CDA = 90°$	4. Definition of an altitude.
5. $m\angle BDA = m\angle CDA$	5. Substitution of equals.
6. $AD = AD$	6. Any quantity is equal to itself.
7. $\therefore \triangle ABD$ and $\triangle ACD$ are congruent.	7. SAS Postulate.

Directions   Write the reason for each statement.

Given: Figure $ABCD$ is a square with diagonal $\overline{BD}$.
To Prove: $\triangle ABD \cong \triangle CBD$

Statement	Reason
1. $AB = BC$	_____
2. $AD = DC$	_____
3. $m\angle A = m\angle C$	_____
4. $\triangle ABD \cong \triangle CBD$	_____

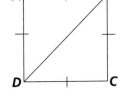

Given: Figure $ABCD$ is a parallelogram with diagonal $\overline{BD}$.
To Prove: $\triangle ABD \cong \triangle CDB$

Statement	Reason
5. $AB = CD$	_____
6. $AD = CB$	_____
7. $\overline{AB}$ is parallel to $\overline{CD}$.	_____
8. $m\angle ABC + m\angle C = 180°$	_____
9. $\overline{AD}$ is parallel to $\overline{BC}$.	_____
10. $m\angle A + m\angle ABC = 180°$	_____

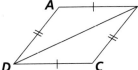

Finish the proof on a separate sheet of paper with statements and reasons.

Proving Triangles Congruent by SSS

EXAMPLE   Use the SSS postulate to prove given triangles are congruent.
Given: *ABCD* is a square with diagonal $\overline{AC}$.
To Prove: $\triangle ABC \cong \triangle ADC$

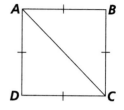

Statement	Reason
1. *AB* = *DC*	1. Definition of a square.
2. *AD* = *BC*	2. Definition of a square.
3. *AC* = *AC*	3. Any quantity is equal to itself.
4. $\triangle ABC \cong \triangle ADC$	4. SSS Postulate.

Directions   Write the reason for each statement.

Given: Figure *ABCD* is a parallelogram with diagonal $\overline{AC}$.
To Prove: $\triangle ABC \cong \triangle ADC$

Statement	Reason
1. *AB* = *CD*	_____
2. *AD* = *BC*	_____
3. *AC* = *AC*	_____
4. $\triangle ABC \cong \triangle ADC$	_____

Given: Figure *ABC* is an isosceles triangle with perpendicular bisector $\overline{AD}$.
To Prove: $\triangle ABD \cong \triangle ACD$

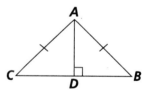

Statement	Reason
5. *AB* = *AC*	_____
6. *AD* = *AD*	_____
7. m$\angle ADB$ = 90°	_____
8. m$\angle ADC$ = 90°	_____
9. $\triangle ABD$ is a right triangle.	_____
10. $(AB)^2 = (AD)^2 + (BD)^2$	_____

Finish the proof on a separate sheet of paper with statements and reasons.

Proving Triangles Congruent by ASA

EXAMPLE   Prove that the given triangles are congruent using the ASA postulate.

Given: Figure ABC is an isosceles triangle. $\overline{AD}$ bisects $\angle A$ and is perpendicular to $\overline{BC}$.

To Prove: $\triangle ABD \cong \triangle ACD$

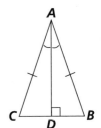

Statement	Reason
1. $\overline{AD}$ bisects $\angle A$.	**1.** Given.
2. $m\angle BAD = m\angle CAD$	**2.** Definition of a bisector.
3. $\overline{AD}$ is perpendicular to $\overline{BC}$.	**3.** Given.
4. $m\angle ADB = 90°$	**4.** Definition of a perpendicular.
5. $m\angle ADC = 90°$	**5.** Definition of a perpendicular.
6. $m\angle ADB = m\angle ADC$	**6.** Substitution of equals.
7. $AD = AD$	**7.** Any quantity is equal to itself.
8. $\triangle ABD \cong \triangle ACD$	**8.** ASA Postulate.

Directions   Write the reason for each statement.

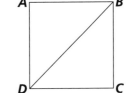

Given: Figure ABCD is a square with diagonal $\overline{BD}$.

To Prove: $\triangle ABD \cong \triangle CDB$

Statement	Reason
1. $\overline{AB}$ is parallel to $\overline{CD}$.	_____
2. $\overline{BD}$ is a transversal of $\overline{AB}$ and $\overline{CD}$.	_____
3. $m\angle ABD = m\angle BDC$	_____
4. $\overline{AD}$ is parallel to $\overline{BC}$.	_____
5. $\overline{BD}$ is a transversal of $\overline{AD}$ and $\overline{BC}$.	_____
6. $m\angle ADB = m\angle DBC$	_____
7. $DB = DB$	_____
8. $\triangle ABD \cong \triangle CDB$	_____

Hypotenuse-Leg Theorem

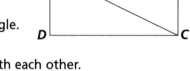

EXAMPLE   Prove that two triangles are congruent using the Hypotenuse-Leg Theorem.

Given: Figure *ABCD* is a rectangle with diagonal $\overline{AC}$.

To Prove: $\triangle ABC \cong \triangle ADC$

Statement	Reason
1. $\angle D$ is a right angle.	1. Given: definition of a rectangle.
2. $\angle B$ is a right angle.	2. Definition of a rectangle.
3. $m\angle D = m\angle B$	3. All right angles are equal with each other.
4. $AB = CD$	4. Given: definition of a rectangle.
5. $AC = AC$	5. Any quantity is equal to itself.
6. $\triangle ABC \cong \triangle ADC$	6. H-L Theorem.

Directions   Write the reason for each statement.

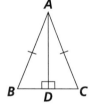

Given: Figure *ABC* is an isosceles triangle with altitude $\overline{AD}$.

To Prove: $\triangle ABD \cong \triangle ACD$

Statement	Reason
1. $AB = AC$	_____
2. $AD = AD$	_____
3. $\angle ADB$ is a right angle.	_____
4. $\angle ADC$ is a right angle.	_____
5. $m\angle ADB = m\angle ADC$	_____
6. $\triangle ABD \cong \triangle ACD$	_____

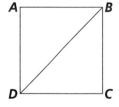

Given: Figure *ABCD* is a square with diagonal $\overline{BD}$.

To Prove: $\triangle ABD \cong \triangle CBD$

Statement	Reason
7. $AB = CD$	_____
8. $BD = BD$	_____
9. $\angle A$ is a right angle.	_____
10. $\angle C$ is a right angle.	_____

Finish the proof with statements and reasons.

Reflections

EXAMPLE

Reflect the image over the *x*-axis.

Reflected points:

$A' = (0, -2)$

$B' = (5, -2)$

$C' = (3, -5)$

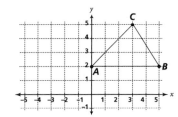

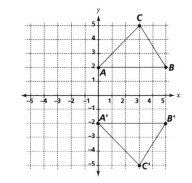

Directions Reflect each image over the specified axis. Give the coordinates of the image vertices. Graph and label the reflected points.

1. Line of reflection = *x*-axis

_____

2. Line of reflection = *y*-axis

_____

3. Line of reflection = *x*-axis

_____

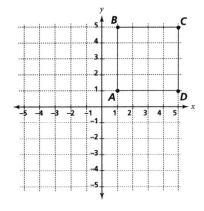

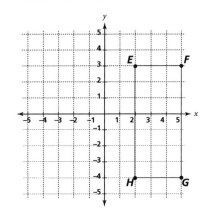

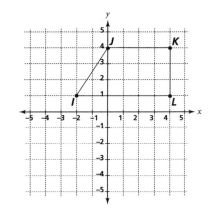

4. Line of reflection = *x*-axis

_____

5. Line of reflection = *y*-axis

_____

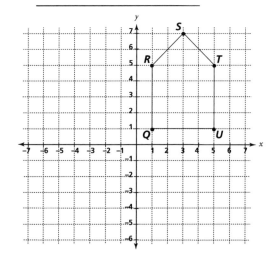

Reflections Over Different Lines

EXAMPLE   Reflect the image over the specified line of reflection: $x = 2$
Give the coordinates of the image vertices.

Reflected points:

$A' = (1, 3)$

$B' = (-1, 3)$

$C' = (-1, 1)$

$D' = (1, 1)$

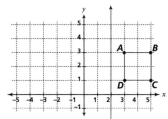

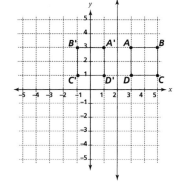

Directions   Reflect each image over the specified line of reflection. Give the
coordinates of the image vertices. Graph and label the reflected points.

1. Line of reflection $x = 3$
_____

2. Line of reflection $y = 1$
_____

3. Line of reflection $x = -1$
_____

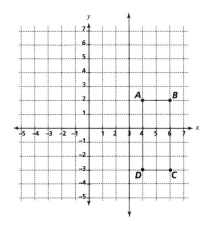

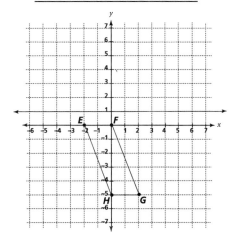

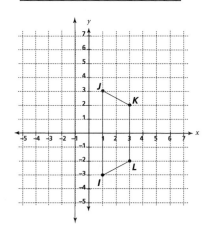

4. Line of reflection $x = 2$
_____

5. Line of reflection $y = -2$
_____

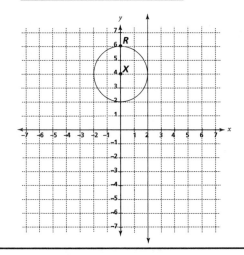

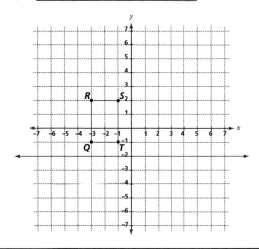

Name Date Period

Workbook Activity 70
Chapter 6, Lesson 6

Alphabet Symmetry

EXAMPLE

Find the line of symmetry in the letter *A*.

A

The letter *A* has a vertical line of symmetry.

A

Directions Draw any lines of symmetry that the following letters have.

1. Y

2. M

3. O

4. B

5. D

6. W

7. X

8. C

9. F

10. H

Identifying Image Translations

EXAMPLE	Name the image point when the object point (3, 4) is mapped by the following translation.

$$(x, y) \rightarrow (x - 2, y - 5)$$

Image point = (1, −1)

Directions Name the image point when the object point (4, 4) is mapped by the following translations.

1. $(x, y) \rightarrow (x - 4, y + 2)$ _____

2. $(x, y) \rightarrow (x + 1, y - 1)$ _____

3. $(x, y) \rightarrow (x - 6, y - 3)$ _____

4. $(x, y) \rightarrow (x + 3, y + 1)$ _____

Directions Name the image point when the object point (−2, 1) is mapped by the following translations.

5. $(x, y) \rightarrow (x - 2, y + 1)$ _____

6. $(x, y) \rightarrow (x - 5, y - 1)$ _____

7. $(x, y) \rightarrow (x + 4, y + 3)$ _____

8. $(x, y) \rightarrow (x - 2, y + 3)$ _____

Directions Name the image point when the object point (−7, 3) is mapped by the following translations.

9. $(x, y) \rightarrow (x + 24, y - 4)$ _____

10. $(x, y) \rightarrow (x - 1, y - 1)$ _____

11. $(x, y) \rightarrow (x + 5, y - 3)$ _____

12. $(x, y) \rightarrow (x - 3, y + 1)$ _____

Directions Identify the image of (x, y) under the following translations. Remember, the image takes the form $(x + a, y + b)$.

13. $(-4, 5) \rightarrow (-6, 2)$ _____

14. $(1, 2) \rightarrow (4, 8)$ _____

15. $(-2, -3) \rightarrow (3, 4)$ _____

Rotating Images

EXAMPLE   Rotate the following image 90° clockwise
around point *O*.

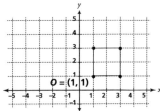

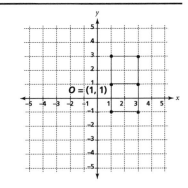

Directions   Copy the given figure onto graph paper. Then rotate the object 90° clockwise
around point *O* to produce an image. Draw the image.

1.

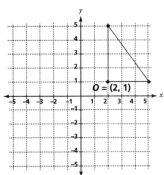

2.

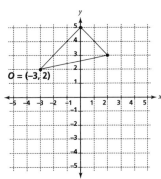

3.

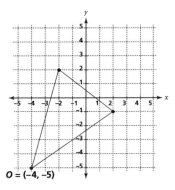

4.

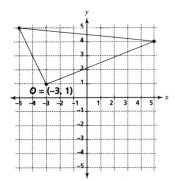

5.

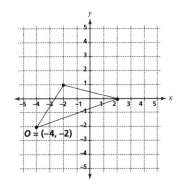

Algebra Connection: Quadratic Equations

EXAMPLE

Solve $x^2 + 2x - 8 = 0$ for x.

Step 1 Factor $x^2 + 2x - 8$. Think: $(4) \cdot (-2) = -8$ and $4 + (-2) = 2$
$x^2 + 2x - 8 = (x + 4)(x - 2) = 0$

Step 2 Set each factor equal to 0 and solve.
$x + 4 = 0 \rightarrow x = -4$ or $x - 2 = 0 \rightarrow x = 2$

Step 3 Check both solutions.
$(-4)^2 + 2 \cdot (-4) - 8 = 16 - 8 - 8 = 0$ $(2)^2 + 2 \cdot 2 - 8 = 4 + 4 - 8 = 0$

Directions Solve these quadratic equations. Check your answers.

1. $x^2 + x - 12 = 0$ _____

2. $y^2 + 11y + 30 = 0$ _____

3. $m^2 + 4m - 5 = 0$ _____

4. $n^2 - 9n + 14 = 0$ _____

5. $c^2 + 5c - 24 = 0$ _____

6. $a^2 - 7a + 10 = 0$ _____

7. $b^2 + 3b - 18 = 0$ _____

8. $z^2 + 5z - 6 = 0$ _____

EXAMPLE

Solve $3x^2 + x - 4 = 0$ for x.

Step 1 Factor. The only possible first terms are $3x$ and x.
The possible second terms are 1 and -4, 4 and -1, or 2 and -2.
$(3x + 4)(x - 1)$ gives the correct middle term: $-3x + 4x = x$.
$3x^2 + x - 4 = (3x + 4)(x - 1) = 0$

Step 2 Set each factor equal to 0 and solve.
$3x + 4 = 0 \rightarrow x = -\frac{4}{3}$ or $x - 1 = 0 \rightarrow x = 1$

Step 3 Check both solutions.
$3 \cdot (-\frac{4}{3})^2 + (-\frac{4}{3}) - 4 = \frac{16}{3} - \frac{4}{3} - \frac{12}{3} = 0$
$3 \cdot (1)^2 + (1) - 4 = 3 + 1 - 4 = 0$

Directions Solve these quadratic equations. Check your answers.

9. $3x^2 - 3x - 36 = 0$ _____

10. $2z^2 - 13z + 15 = 0$ _____

11. $3w^2 + 18w + 15 = 0$ _____

12. $3w^2 + 12w - 15 = 0$ _____

13. $5y^2 + 4y - 12 = 0$ _____

14. $3x^2 + 2x - 8 = 0$ _____

15. $3x^2 - 2x - 8 = 0$ _____

Proportions

EXAMPLE

Find the missing value in the following proportion.

$$\frac{10}{15} = \frac{20}{x}$$

The outside elements, the 10 and the x, are called the *extremes*. The inside elements, the 15 and the 20, are called the *means*.

The theorem states that the product of the extremes = the product of the means. Write the following equation.

10x = 300   Divide both sides by 10 to get x = 30.

Directions Find the missing value in each proportion.

1. $\frac{3}{4} = \frac{x}{12}$ _____

2. $\frac{5}{8} = \frac{10}{x}$ _____

3. $\frac{11}{23} = \frac{44}{x}$ _____

4. $\frac{x}{3} = \frac{3}{9}$ _____

5. $\frac{7}{x} = \frac{12}{24}$ _____

6. $\frac{5}{x} = \frac{20}{24}$ _____

7. $\frac{2}{5} = \frac{8}{x}$ _____

8. $\frac{8}{13} = \frac{24}{x}$ _____

9. $\frac{x}{34} = \frac{11}{33}$ _____

10. $\frac{5}{9} = \frac{x}{27}$ _____

11. $\frac{19}{x} = \frac{20}{25}$ _____

12. $\frac{33}{33} = \frac{x}{24}$ _____

13. $\frac{8}{15} = \frac{x}{30}$ _____

14. $\frac{x}{60} = \frac{10}{24}$ _____

15. $\frac{4}{x} = \frac{12}{26}$ _____

Determining Equal Ratios

EXAMPLE Determine if the following ratios are equal to each other. Use the theorem that the product of the extremes equals the product of the means.

$\frac{5}{3}$ and $\frac{25}{9}$

The product of the extremes, 5 and 9, is 45.

The product of the means, 3 and 25, is 75.

Since the product of the means must equal the product of the extremes in order for two ratios to be equal, these two ratios are not equal.

Directions Are the following ratios equal? Write *Yes* or *No*. Use the theorem that the product of the extremes equals the product of the means.

1. $\frac{5}{8}$ and $\frac{7}{10}$ _____

2. $\frac{6}{10}$ and $\frac{12}{20}$ _____

3. $\frac{8}{3}$ and $\frac{24}{9}$ _____

4. $\frac{2}{5}$ and $\frac{10}{25}$ _____

5. $\frac{9}{4}$ and $\frac{17}{8}$ _____

6. $\frac{35}{40}$ and $\frac{7}{8}$ _____

7. $\frac{10}{1}$ and $\frac{30}{1}$ _____

8. $\frac{15}{16}$ and $\frac{17}{18}$ _____

9. $\frac{21}{24}$ and $\frac{14}{16}$ _____

10. $\frac{60}{66}$ and $\frac{10}{11}$ _____

11. $\frac{99}{100}$ and $\frac{9}{10}$ _____

12. $\frac{85}{50}$ and $\frac{17}{10}$ _____

13. $\frac{6}{3}$ and $\frac{7}{4}$ _____

14. $\frac{9}{16}$ and $\frac{27}{48}$ _____

15. $\frac{36}{60}$ and $\frac{6}{10}$ _____

Corresponding Angles and Sides

EXAMPLE	Name the corresponding angles and sides of the similar triangles.

$m\angle BAC = ?$ $m\angle EDC$

$m\angle ABC = ?$ $m\angle DEC$

$m\angle ACB = ?$ $m\angle DCE$

$\frac{AB}{?} = \frac{BC}{?}$ $\overline{DE}, \overline{EC}$

$\frac{BC}{?} = \frac{AC}{?}$ $\overline{EC}, \overline{DC}$

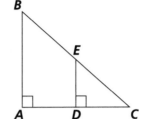

Directions Name the corresponding angles and sides of the similar triangles.

1. $m\angle P = ?$ _____

2. $m\angle Q = ?$ _____

3. $m\angle PRQ = ?$ _____

4. $\frac{QP}{?} = \frac{QR}{?}$ _____

5. $\frac{PR}{?} = \frac{QP}{?}$ _____

6. $m\angle A = ?$ _____

7. $m\angle B = ?$ _____

8. $m\angle C = ?$ _____

9. $\frac{AB}{?} = \frac{BC}{?}$ _____

10. $\frac{AC}{?} = \frac{AB}{?}$ _____

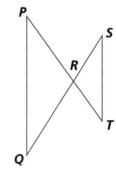

11. $m\angle A = ?$ _____

12. $m\angle B = ?$ _____

13. $m\angle C = ?$ _____

14. $\frac{AB}{?} = \frac{BC}{?}$ _____

15. $\frac{AC}{?} = \frac{AB}{?}$ _____

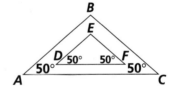

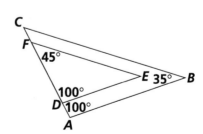

Name _____ Date _____ Period _____

Using the AA Postulate

EXAMPLE   Solve for the values of the unknowns
in this pair of similar triangles.

x = ?   8

y = ?   20

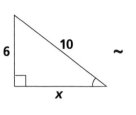 ~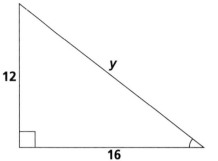

Directions   Each pair of triangles is similar. Solve for the values of the unknowns.

1. x = ? _____

2. y = ? _____

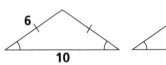 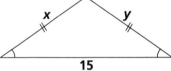

3. m∠BAD = ? _____

4. m∠DAC = ? _____

5. AC = ? _____

6. AD = ? _____

7. DC = ? _____

8. BD = ? _____

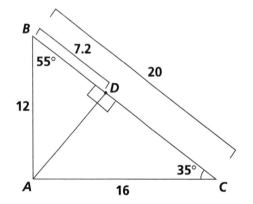

9. DF = ? _____

10. EF = ? _____

11. AD = ? _____

12. AE = ? _____

13. BC = ? _____

14. EC = ? _____

15. height of ΔABC = ? _____

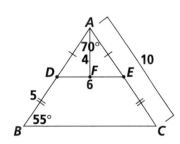

The Ratio of Similarity

EXAMPLE   The ratio of similarity can be used to find the perimeters
of similar nonregular polygons.

Given: The ratio of similarity between the two triangles is 1:3.

Find the perimeter of the larger polygon.

Use the ratio of similarity to find the measure of the larger
triangle's sides: 9, 12, and 15. The sum of these is 36.
Calculate the perimeter of the smaller triangle first, which
is 12. If you use the ratio of similarity with the smaller
triangle's perimeter, you get 36 as well.

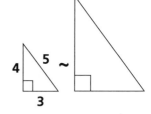

Directions   Use the ratio of similarity to find the perimeter of the larger polygon.

1. The ratio of similarity is 1:4.

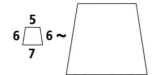

_____

2. The ratio of similarity is 3:4.

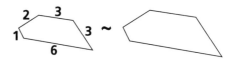

_____

3. The ratio of similarity is 2:3.

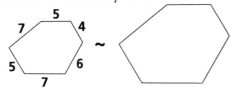

_____

4. The ratio of similarity is 3:5.

_____

5. The ratio of similarity is 5:8.

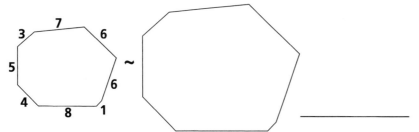

_____

Angle Measure in Regular Polygons

EXAMPLE The measure of an interior angle of a regular polygon = $180° - \frac{360°}{n}$
where n = number of sides.

regular octagon ($n = 8$)

angle measure = $180° - \frac{360°}{8} = 180° - 45° = 135°$

Directions Find the measure of each interior angle for a regular polygon with the given number of sides. Use the formula to calculate the measure.

1.

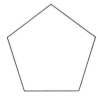

_____

2.

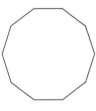

_____

3.

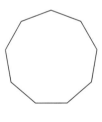

_____

4.

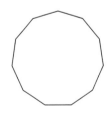

_____

5.

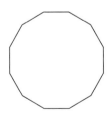

_____

Finding the Ratio of Similarity

EXAMPLE   Find the ratio of similarity. It can be used to find the lengths of missing sides.

$\frac{\text{base of smaller triangle}}{\text{base of larger triangle}} = \frac{6}{12} = \frac{1}{2}$

hypotenuse of smaller triangle = 10

hyopotenuse of larger triangle = x

$\frac{1}{2} = \frac{10}{x}$ $x = 20$

leg of smaller triangle = 8

leg of larger triangle = y

$\frac{8}{y} = \frac{1}{2}$ $y = 16$

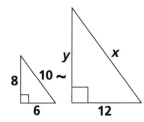

Directions   Find the ratio of similarity in the following pairs of similar figures.

1. _____

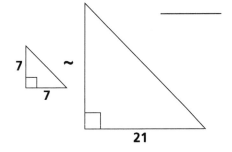

2. _____

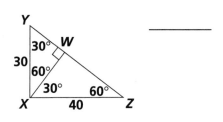

3. _____

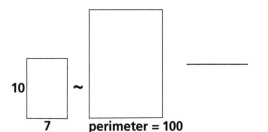

4. _____

5. _____

Dilating Images

EXAMPLE

Give the coordinates of the image under the following dilation. Use graph paper to graph the object and its image. (All dilations have (0, 0) as the center of the dilation.)

Graph the image after dilating it by 3.

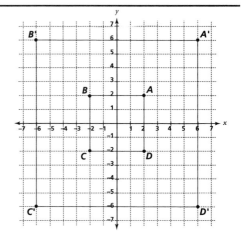

$A' = 3 \bullet (2, 2) = (3 \bullet 2, 3 \bullet 2) = (6, 6)$

$B' = 3 \bullet (-2, 2) = (3 \bullet -2, 3 \bullet 2) = (-6, 6)$

$C' = 3 \bullet (-2, -2) = (3 \bullet -2, 3 \bullet -2) = (-6, -6)$

$D' = 3 \bullet (2, -2) = (3 \bullet 2, 3 \bullet -2) = (6, -6)$

Directions   Give the coordinates of the image under the following dilations. Use graph paper to graph each object and its images. (All dilations have $(0, 0)$ as the center of the dilation.)

1. dilation of 2   _____   **6.** dilation of 2   _____

2. dilation of 3   _____   **7.** dilation of 3   _____

3. dilation of 4   _____   **8.** dilation of 4   _____

4. dilation of 5   _____   **9.** dilation of 5   _____

5. dilation of 6   _____   **10.** dilation of 6   _____

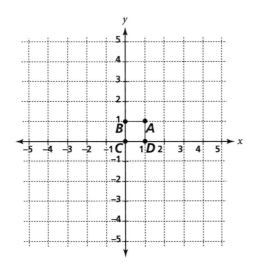

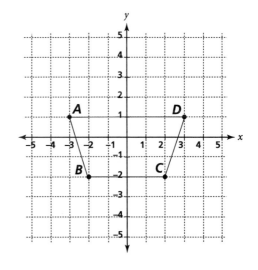

More Dilations

EXAMPLE   Give the coordinates of the image under the
following dilation. Use graph paper to graph
the object and its image. (All dilations have
(0, 0) as the center of the dilation.)

Give the image after dilating it by 2.

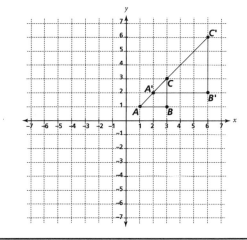

$A' = 2 \cdot (1, 1) = (2 \cdot 1, 2 \cdot 1) = (2, 2)$

$B' = 2 \cdot (3, 1) = (2 \cdot 3, 2 \cdot 1) = (6, 2)$

$C' = 2 \cdot (3, 3) = (2 \cdot 3, 2 \cdot 3) = (6, 6)$

Directions   Give the coordinates of the image under the following dilations.
Use graph paper to graph each object and its images.
(All dilations have (0, 0) as the center of the dilation.)

1. dilation of 2   _____

2. dilation of 3   _____

3. dilation of 4   _____

4. dilation of 5   _____

5. dilation of 6   _____

6. dilation of 2   _____

7. dilation of 3   _____

8. dilation of 4   _____

9. dilation of 5   _____

10. dilation of 6   _____

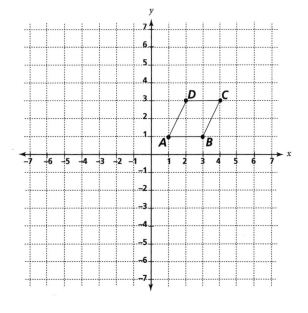

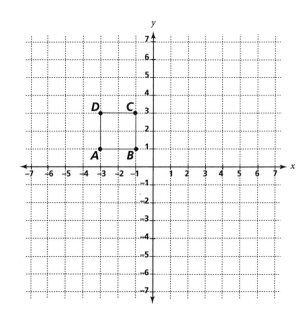

Shrinking Images

EXAMPLE

Give the coordinates of the image under the following dilation. Use graph paper to graph the object and its image. (All dilations have (0, 0) as the center of the dilation.)

Graph the image after dilating it by $\frac{3}{5}$.

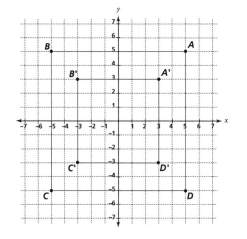

$A' = \frac{3}{5} \bullet (5, 5) = (\frac{3}{5} \bullet 5, \frac{3}{5} \bullet 5) = (3, 3)$

$B' = \frac{3}{5} \bullet (-5, 5) = (\frac{3}{5} \bullet -5, \frac{3}{5} \bullet 5) = (-3, 3)$

$C' = \frac{3}{5} \bullet (-5, -5) = (\frac{3}{5} \bullet -5, \frac{3}{5} \bullet -5) = (-3, -3)$

$D' = \frac{3}{5} \bullet (5, -5) = (\frac{3}{5} \bullet 5, \frac{3}{5} \bullet -5) = (3, -3)$

Directions Give the coordinates of the image under the following dilations. Use graph paper to graph each object and its images. (All dilations have (0, 0) as the center of the dilation.)

1. dilation of $\frac{1}{2}$ _____

2. dilation of $\frac{1}{3}$ _____

3. dilation of $\frac{1}{4}$ _____

4. dilation of $\frac{1}{5}$ _____

5. dilation of $\frac{1}{6}$ _____

6. dilation of $\frac{5}{6}$ _____

7. dilation of $\frac{2}{3}$ _____

8. dilation of $\frac{1}{2}$ _____

9. dilation of $\frac{1}{3}$ _____

10. dilation of $\frac{1}{6}$ _____

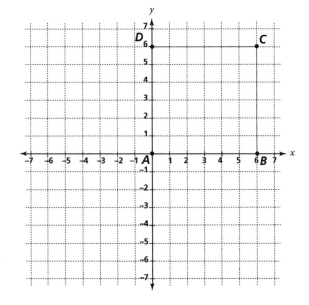

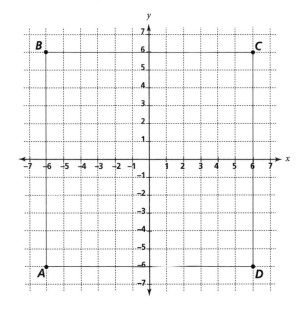

More Shrinking

EXAMPLE Give the coordinates of the image under the following dilation. Use graph paper to graph the object and its image. (All dilations have (0, 0) as the center of the dilation.)

Graph the image after dilating it by $\frac{1}{5}$.

$A' = \frac{1}{5} \bullet (2, 2) = (\frac{1}{5} \bullet 2, \frac{1}{5} \bullet 2) = (\frac{2}{5}, \frac{2}{5})$

$B' = \frac{1}{5} \bullet (6, 2) = (\frac{1}{5} \bullet 6, \frac{1}{5} \bullet 2) = (\frac{6}{5}, \frac{2}{5})$

$C' = \frac{1}{5} \bullet (6, 10) = (\frac{1}{5} \bullet 6, \frac{1}{5} \bullet 10) = (\frac{6}{5}, 2)$

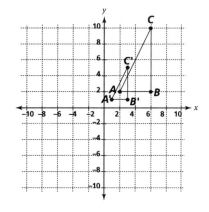

Directions Give the coordinates of the image under the following dilations. Use graph paper to graph each object and its images. (All dilations have (0, 0) as the center of the dilation.)

1. dilation of $\frac{1}{2}$ _____

2. dilation of $\frac{2}{3}$ _____

3. dilation of $\frac{3}{4}$ _____

4. dilation of $\frac{4}{5}$ _____

5. dilation of $\frac{5}{6}$ _____

6. dilation of $\frac{1}{5}$ _____

7. dilation of $\frac{2}{5}$ _____

8. dilation of $\frac{3}{5}$ _____

9. dilation of $\frac{4}{5}$ _____

10. dilation of $\frac{1}{10}$ _____

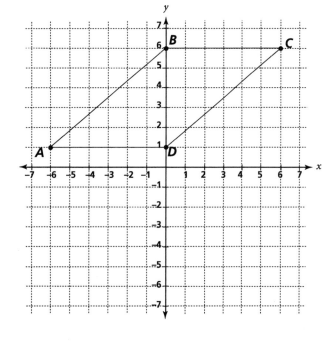

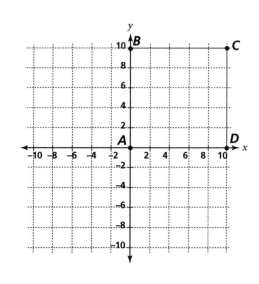

Algebra Connection: The Counting Principle

EXAMPLE	Jenna has four shirts, three pairs of pants, and five different pairs of socks. How many different combinations of shirts, pants, and socks can she wear? Multiply the number of choices. 4 • 3 • 5 = 60 Jenna can wear 60 different combinations of shirts, pants and socks.

Directions   Solve.

1. Suppose five different roads go from *A* to *B* and eight different roads go from *B* to *C*. How many ways can you go from *A* to *B* to *C*?   _____

2. Jon has eight shirts, three sweaters, and six pairs of pants. How many different combinations of shirts, sweaters, and pants can he wear?   _____

3. A test has eight true/false questions. How many arrangements of answers are possible?   _____

EXAMPLE	Hamilton, Annie, Joshua, and Sunita line up for a picture. How many different ways can they line up? There are 4 choices for first place, 3 choices for second place, 2 choices for third place, and 1 choice for fourth place. 4 • 3 • 2 • 1 = 24 They can line up 24 different ways.

Directions   Solve.

4. How many different ways can four people line up for a picture?   _____

5. How many different ways can six people line up for a picture?   _____

6. How many different ways can ten people line up for a picture?   _____

EXAMPLE	Find 6! 6! = 6 • 5 • 4 • 3 • 2 • 1 = 720

Directions   Write each factorial as a product. Then find the product. You may use a calculator.

7. 2! _____   **9.** 9! _____

8. 7! _____   **10.** 12! _____

Checking Triples

EXAMPLE   Check if the given set of numbers is a Pythagorean Triple. Use a calculator.
       125, 300, 325

In order to check if a given set of numbers is a Pythagorean Triple, you must use the Pythagorean Theorem. If the sum of the squares of the two smaller numbers equals the square of the largest number, then the set of numbers is a Pythagorean Triple.

This can be expressed in the equation $a^2 + b^2 = c^2$.

You can now write the equation $125^2 + 300^2 = 325^2$.

This can be reduced to $15{,}625 + 90{,}000 = 105{,}625$.

Since this equation is true, the number set is a Pythagorean Triple.

Directions   Check if the given sets of numbers are Pythagorean Triples. Write *Yes* or *No*. Use a calculator.

1. (4, 5, 6) _____

2. (14, 15, 16) _____

3. (6, 8, 10) _____

4. (45, 79, 83) _____

5. (20, 399, 401) _____

6. (12, 35, 37) _____

7. (31, 225, 227) _____

8. (30, 72, 78) _____

9. (22, 27, 34) _____

10. (60, 80, 100) _____

11. (35, 84, 91) _____

12. (18, 25, 30) _____

13. (20, 47, 56) _____

14. (25, 60, 65) _____

15. (14, 21, 26) _____

Plato's Formula

EXAMPLE   Use Plato's Formula to find a Pythagorean Triple for the given integer.
Use a calculator. $m = 7$

Plato's Formula is $(2m)^2 + (m^2 - 1)^2 = (m^2 + 1)^2$

$$(2 \cdot 7)^2 + (7^2 - 1)^2 = (7^2 + 1)^2$$

$$14^2 + 48^2 = 50^2$$

The square roots of these numbers gives you a number set of 14, 48, and 50.

Check by squaring the numbers. If the equation is true, then the numbers
are a Pythagorean Triple. $196 + 2{,}304 = 2{,}500$
Since $196 + 2{,}304$ equals $2{,}500$, the numbers 14, 48, and 50 are a
Pythagorean Triple.

Directions   Use Plato's Formula to find Pythagorean Triples for the
given integers. Use a calculator.

1. $m = 4$ _____

2. $m = 5$ _____

3. $m = 8$ _____

4. $m = 9$ _____

5. $m = 11$ _____

6. $m = 12$ _____

7. $m = 13$ _____

8. $m = 14$ _____

9. $m = 16$ _____

10. $m = 17$ _____

11. $m = 18$ _____

12. $m = 19$ _____

13. $m = 21$ _____

14. $m = 22$ _____

15. $m = 30$ _____

Pythagorean Triples and Proofs

EXAMPLE Use the figure to find the following quantities:

Area of the large square = 26 • 26 = 676

Area of each triangle = $\frac{1}{2}$(10 • 24) = $\frac{1}{2}$(240) = 120

Area of the small square = 14 • 14 = 196

Sum of the areas that make up the large square =
        120 + 120 + 120 + 120 + 196 = 676

Does the area of the large square equal the sum
of the areas of the four triangles plus the area
of the small square?   Yes

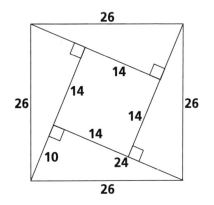

Directions Use the figures to find the following quantities.

1. Area of the large square = _____

2. Area of each triangle = _____

3. Area of the small square = _____

4. Sum of the areas that make up the large square =

   _____

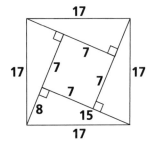

5. Does the area of the large square equal the sum of the areas
   of the four triangles plus the area of the small square? _____

6. Area of the large square = _____

7. Area of each triangle = _____

8. Area of the small square = _____

9. Sum of the areas that make up the large square =

   _____

10. Does the area of the large square equal the sum of the
    areas of the four triangles plus the area of the small
    square? _____

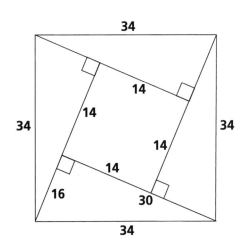

Pythagorean Demonstration

EXAMPLE   What is the area of each right triangle in Square I? 96

What is the length of each side of the inner square in Square I? 20

What is the area of the inner square in Square I? 400

What is the total area of Square I? 784

What is the sum of the areas of the four right triangles plus the area of the inner square?

$$96 + 96 + 96 + 96 + 400 = 784$$

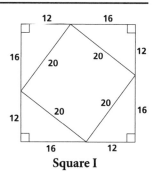

Square I

What is the area of the smaller square in Square II? 144

What is the area of the larger inside square in Square II? 256

What is the area of each rectangle in Square II? 192

What is the sum of the areas of the squares plus the areas of the rectangles? $144 + 256 + 192 + 192 = 784$

How does the area of Square I compare to the area of Square II?   They are equal.

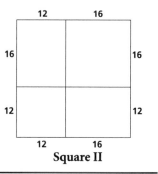

Square II

Directions   Use the figures to answer the questions.

1. What is the area of each right triangle in Square I? _____

2. What is the length of each side of the inner square in Square I? _____

3. What is the area of the inner square in Square I? _____

4. What is the total area of Square I? _____

5. What is the sum of the areas of the four right triangles plus the area of the inner square? _____

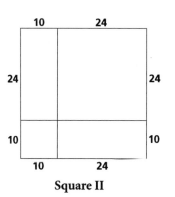

Square I

6. What is the area of the smaller square in Square II?   _____

7. What is the area of the larger inside square in Square II?   _____

8. What is the area of each rectangle in Square II? _____

9. What is the sum of the areas of the squares plus the areas of the rectangles? _____

10. How does the area of Square I compare to the area of Square II?

_____

Square II

Pythagorean Theorem and Similar Triangles

EXAMPLE ΔABC is similar to both ΔDBA and ΔDAC.

ΔDBA is similar to ΔDAC.

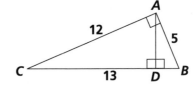

Directions Use the figure to answer the following questions.

1. What is the length of $\overline{WZ}$? _____

2. What is the length of $\overline{XZ}$? _____

3. What is the length of $\overline{YZ}$? _____

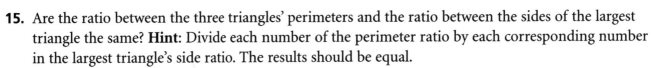

4. What segment makes up the hypotenuse of the largest triangle? _____

5. What segment makes up the hypotenuse of the middle-sized triangle? _____

6. What segment makes up the hypotenuse of the smallest triangle? _____

7. Is ΔWXZ similar to ΔWYZ? Why? _____

8. What is the ratio of similarity between ΔWXY and ΔZXW? _____

9. What is the ratio of similarity between ΔWXY and ΔZWY? _____

10. What is the ratio of similarity between ΔZXW and ΔZWY? _____

11. What is the perimeter of ΔWXY? _____

12. What is the perimeter of ΔZWY? _____

13. What is the perimeter of ΔZXW? _____

14. What is the ratio between the three triangles' perimeters? _____

15. Are the ratio between the three triangles' perimeters and the ratio between the sides of the largest triangle the same? **Hint:** Divide each number of the perimeter ratio by each corresponding number in the largest triangle's side ratio. The results should be equal.

_____

More with Similar Triangles

EXAMPLE   △ABC is similar to both △DAB and △DAC.

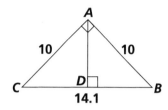

Directions   Use the figure to answer the following questions.

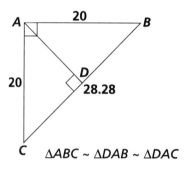

△ABC ~ △DAB ~ △DAC

1. What is the length of $\overline{AD}$?   _____

2. What is the length of $\overline{BD}$?   _____

3. What is the length of $\overline{CD}$?   _____

4. What segment makes up the hypotenuse of the largest triangle?

_____

5. What segment makes up the hypotenuse of the left smaller triangle?   _____

6. What segment makes up the hypotenuse of the right smaller triangle?   _____

7. Is △DAB similar to △DAC? Why? _____

8. What is the ratio of similarity between △ABC and △DAB?   _____

9. What is the ratio of similarity between △ABC and △DAC?   _____

10. What is the ratio of similarity between △DAB and △DAC?   _____

11. What is the perimeter of △ABC?   _____

12. What is the perimeter of △DAB?   _____

13. What is the perimeter of △DAC?   _____

14. What is the ratio between the three triangles' perimeters?   _____

15. Are the ratio between the three triangles' perimeters and the ratio between the sides of the largest triangle the same? **Hint:** Divide each number of the perimeter ratio by each corresponding number in the largest triangle's side ratio. The results should be equal.

_____

Special Triangles

EXAMPLE One side of an equilateral triangle is 5 cm. What are the other sides?
The ratio of the sides of an equilateral triangle is 1:1:1.
Multiply the ratio by 5. $5 \cdot 1{:}5 \cdot 1{:}5 \cdot 1 \rightarrow 5{:}5{:}5$
The other sides are 5 cm and 5 cm.

Directions One side of an equilateral triangle is given. Solve for the other sides.
You may leave your answer in square root form.

1. 2 ft   _____   **4.** 8.5 in.   _____

2. 7 in.   _____   **5.** 100 yd   _____

3. 9 cm   _____

EXAMPLE $\triangle ABC$ is an isosceles right triangle. Each leg is 3 in.
Find the hypotenuse. The ratio of the sides is $1{:}1{:}\sqrt{2}$.
Multiply each number by 3. $(3 \cdot 1){:}(3 \cdot 1){:}(3 \cdot \sqrt{2}) = 3{:}3{:}3\sqrt{2}$.
The hypotenuse is $3\sqrt{2}$ in.

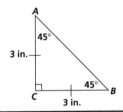

Directions One leg of an isosceles right triangle is given. Solve for the hypotenuse.
You may leave your answer in square root form

6. 4 units _____ **10.** $\frac{1}{2}$ ft _____

7. 8 cm _____ **11.** $\frac{3}{8}$ mi _____

8. 9 m _____ **12.** 9.5 in. _____

9. 13 km _____

EXAMPLE The hypotenuse of a 30°-60° right triangle is 2 units.
What are the lengths of the two legs?
The ratio of the sides is $1{:}\frac{1}{2}{:}\frac{\sqrt{3}}{2}$. Multiply each number by 2.
$(1 \cdot 2){:}(\frac{1}{2} \cdot 2){:}(\frac{\sqrt{3}}{2} \cdot 2) = 2{:}1{:}\sqrt{3}$
The legs are 1 unit and $\sqrt{3}$ units.

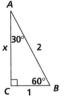

Directions The hypotenuse of a 30°-60° right triangle is given. Solve for both legs.
You may leave your answer in square root form.

13. 6 units _____ **17.** 17 m _____

14. 26 in. _____ **18.** 4.2 mi _____

15. 90 km _____ **19.** 7.4 units _____

16. 19 ft _____ **20.** 18.54 cm _____

Pythagorean Proof and Trapezoids

EXAMPLE Calculate the area of the trapezoid.

The formula for the area of a trapezoid is

area = $\frac{h(a + b)}{2}$ where *a* and *b* are bases and *h* is height.

area = $\frac{5(14 + 16)}{2}$

This can be simplified to $\frac{5(30)}{2}$ = 5 • 15 = 75.

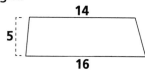

Directions Calculate the area of each trapezoid.

1.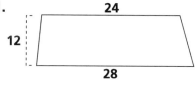

_____

2.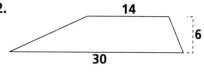

_____

3.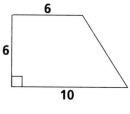

_____

4.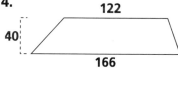

_____

5.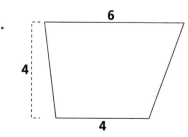

_____

6.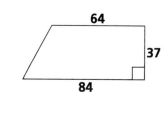

_____

7.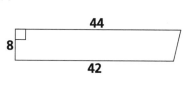

_____

8.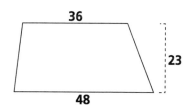

_____

9.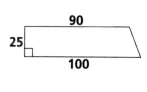

_____

10.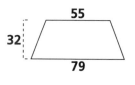

_____

Distance Formula

EXAMPLE Find the distance between the points A and B.
You may leave the distance in square root form.

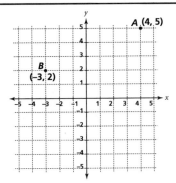

Draw a right triangle with hypotenuse $\overline{AB}$. Then use the Pythagorean Theorem to calculate the distance by writing the equation $(AB)^2 = 7^2 + 3^2$. This can be simplified to $(AB)^2 = 49 + 9 = 58$. Take the square root of both sides to get $AB = \sqrt{58}$.

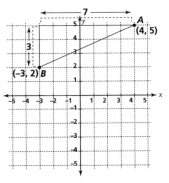

Directions Complete the right triangle to find the distance between the named points. You may leave the distance in square root form.

1. A and B _____

2. A and C _____

3. A and D _____

4. A and E _____

5. B and C _____

6. B and D _____

7. B and E _____

8. C and D _____

9. C and E _____

10. D and E _____

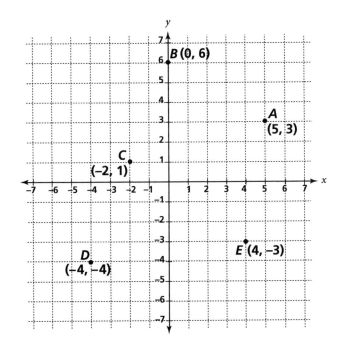

More Distance Formula

EXAMPLE   Use the distance formula to find the distances between the given points.

Given: $A = (0, 8)$ and $B = (-3, 4)$

Distance formula: $d = \sqrt{(x_2 - x_1)^2 + (y_2 - y_1)^2}$

You can write the equation $d = \sqrt{(-3 - 0)^2 + (4 - 8)^2}$.

This can be simplified to $d = \sqrt{(-3)^2 + (-4)^2} = \sqrt{9 + 16} = \sqrt{25} = 5$.

The distance between A and B is 5.

Directions   Use the distance formula to find the distance between the given points. You may leave your distance in square root form.

1. $(3, 2)$ and $(5, 7)$ _____

2. $(-3, 5)$ and $(4, -1)$ _____

3. $(0, 2)$ and $(-1, 4)$ _____

4. $(8, -5)$ and $(3, 6)$ _____

5. $(-6, -3)$ and $(-4, 2)$ _____

6. $(-4, 1)$ and $(5, 5)$ _____

7. $(0, 0)$ and $(7, 7)$ _____

8. $(-4, -5)$ and $(-6, -7)$ _____

9. $(9, 3)$ and $(3, -4)$ _____

10. $(7, 2)$ and $(3, -5)$ _____

11. $(3, -9)$ and $(-12, 4)$ _____

12. $(8, 2)$ and $(-1, 0)$ _____

13. $(8, 8)$ and $(0, 7)$ _____

14. $(2, 3)$ and $(-4, -3)$ _____

15. $(-8, 11)$ and $(-4, 5)$ _____

Name _____ Date _____ Period _____

Converse of the Pythagorean Theorem

EXAMPLE   The converse of the Pythagorean Theorem states that for a triangle to be a right triangle, its sides must conform to the equation $a^2 + b^2 = c^2$. Test this triple: 14, 48, 50

$$14^2 + 48^2 = 50^2$$

If the equation is true, then the triple could be the sides of a right triangle. If we simplify the above statement, we get $196 + 2{,}304 = 2{,}500$. Since this is a true statement, the triple can be the sides of a right triangle.

Directions   Use the converse of the Pythagorean Theorem to test whether these triples are the sides of a right triangle. Answer *Yes* or *No*.

1. 50, 624, 626 _____

2. 80, 1,599, 1,601 _____

3. 3, 6, 8 _____

4. 7, 37, 39 _____

5. 12, 37, 39 _____

6. 21, 109, 111 _____

7. 17, 71.25, 73.25 _____

8. 16, 65, 67 _____

9. 31, 255, 257 _____

10. 24, 143, 145 _____

11. 36, 323, 325 _____

12. 48, 2,303, 2,305 _____

13. 1, 1, 2 _____

14. 50, 625, 627 _____

15. 60, 899, 901 _____

Algebra Connection: Denominators and Zero

EXAMPLE   For what value of x is $\dfrac{5}{x + \frac{3}{8}}$ undefined?

When $x + \dfrac{3}{8} = 0$, the fraction is undefined.

Solve $x + \dfrac{3}{8} = 0$. $x + \dfrac{3}{8} - \dfrac{3}{8} = 0 - \dfrac{3}{8}$ $x = -\dfrac{3}{8}$

When $x = -\dfrac{3}{8}$, the fraction is undefined.

Directions   Find the value for which each fraction is undefined.

1. $\dfrac{1}{y - 7}$ _____

2. $\dfrac{8}{y + 4}$ _____

3. $\dfrac{-13}{c + \frac{1}{2}}$ _____

4. $\dfrac{2a}{3y}$ _____

5. $\dfrac{4x}{x + 20}$ _____

6. $\dfrac{3n}{s - \frac{2}{7}}$ _____

7. $\dfrac{-6}{3m + 3}$ _____

8. $\dfrac{c}{z - \frac{4}{3}}$ _____

9. $\dfrac{4m}{r + 17}$ _____

10. $\dfrac{23p}{q + \frac{7}{8}}$ _____

Directions   Find the values for which each fraction is undefined.

11. $\dfrac{3}{y^2 - 4}$ _____

12. $\dfrac{-3}{m^2 - 64}$ _____

13. $\dfrac{3a}{s^2 - 36}$ _____

14. $\dfrac{29}{25 - x^2}$ _____

15. $\dfrac{1}{(a + 5)(a - 3)}$ _____

16. $\dfrac{a}{z(z + 8)}$ _____

17. $\dfrac{x + 5}{(x - 4)(x + 1)}$ _____

18. $\dfrac{r}{(r - 3)(r + 10)}$ _____

19. $\dfrac{1}{y^2 + 8y + 15}$ _____

20. $\dfrac{w + 3}{w^2 - w - 20}$ _____

Perimeters of Polygons

Find the perimeter of the figure.

The perimeter of a polygon is the sum of the lengths of its sides.

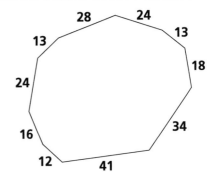

Write the equation.

perimeter = 24 + 13 + 18 + 34 + 41 + 12 + 16 + 24 + 13 + 28

This can be simplified to 223.

Directions Find the perimeter of each figure.

1.

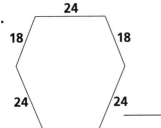

_____

2.

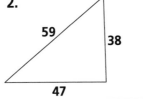

_____

3.

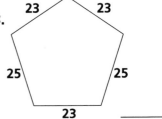

_____

4.

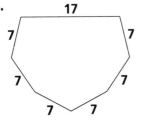

_____

5.

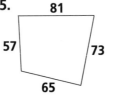

_____

6.

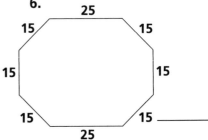

_____

7.

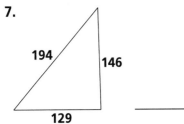

_____

8.

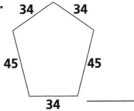

_____

9.

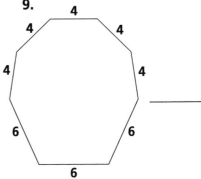

_____

10.

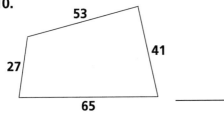

_____

Perimeter Formulas

EXAMPLE	The formula to calculate the perimeter of a rectangle is $P = 2(b + h)$.

You are given a value of 65 for b and a value of 87 for h.

You can write the equation $P = 2(65 + 87)$.

This can be simplified to $P = 2(152) = 304$.

87

65

Directions Use the formula to calculate the perimeter of each rectangle or parallelogram.

1.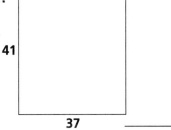
41
37 _____

2.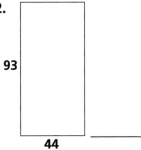
93
44 _____

3.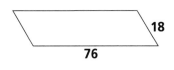
18
76 _____

4.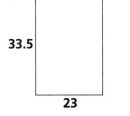
33.5
23 _____

5.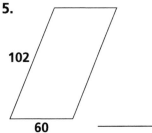
102
60 _____

6.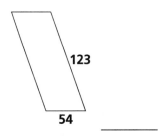
123
54 _____

7.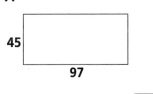
45
97 _____

8.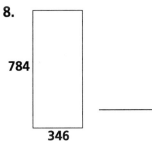
784
346 _____

9.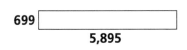
699
5,895 _____

10.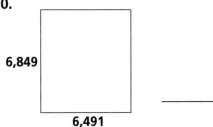
6,849
6,491 _____

Perimeters and Diagonals

EXAMPLE   Use the Pythagorean Theorem to find the perimeter of △ABC.

Calculate the length of $\overline{AC}$. The length of 12 for the base $\overline{DC}$ and 5
for the height $\overline{AD}$ are given. Write the equation:

$(AC)^2 = 12^2 + 5^2$. This can be simplified to $(AC)^2 = 144 + 25 = 169$.

Take the square root of both sides to get $AC = 13$.

You know that the parallel sides of a rectangle are equal. Therefore,
you know that side $\overline{AB}$ is the same length as base $\overline{DC}$, which is 12.
You also know that side $\overline{BC}$ is the same length as height $\overline{AD}$, which is 5.

You can now write an equation for the perimeter of △ABC, $P = 13 + 12 + 5 = 30$.

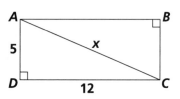

Directions   Use the Pythagorean Theorem to find the missing side. Then calculate
the perimeter. Use a calculator and round to the nearest tenth.

1.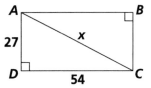

_____

2.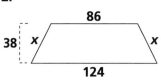

_____

3.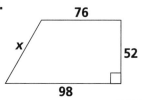

_____

4.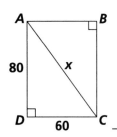

_____

5.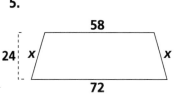

_____

6.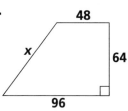

_____

7.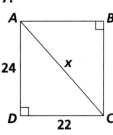

_____

8.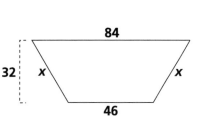

_____

9.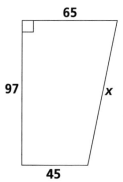

_____

10.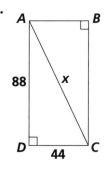

_____

Parallelogram Areas

EXAMPLE   Find the area of the parallelogram.

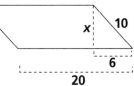

Use the Pythagorean Theorem to find the length of *x*, which is the
height of the parallelogram. The length of 10 for the hypotenuse
of the triangle and a length of 6 for the base are given.

Write the equation $10^2 = 6^2 + x^2$. This can be simplified to $100 = 36 + x^2$.
Subtract 36 from both sides to get $x^2 = 64$. Take the square root of both
sides to get $x = 8$. Now that you have a value of 8 for the height of the
parallelogram, you can write an equation for its area.

area = 20 • 8 = 160

Directions   Find the area of each parallelogram.

1.

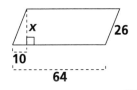

_____

2.

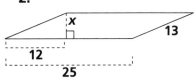

_____

3.

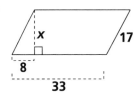

_____

4.

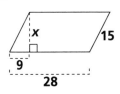

_____

5.

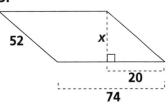

_____

6.

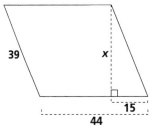

_____

7.

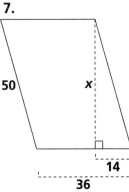

_____

8.

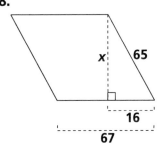

_____

9.

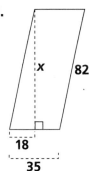

_____

10.

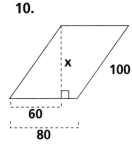

_____

Areas of Trapezoids

EXAMPLE   Use what you know about the area of a trapezoid to find the values
of the average base. The formula for the area of a trapezoid is
area = (*ab*) • (height), where the average base is *ab*.

You are given a value of 300 for the area and 10 for the height.

You can write the equation 300 = *ab* • 10.
Divide both sides by 10 to get *ab* = 30.

10 ⟋ Area = 300

Directions   Use what you know about the area of a trapezoid to find the value
of each unknown.

1.
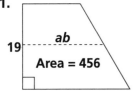
19 *ab*
Area = 456

_____

2.
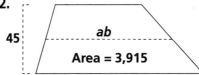
45 *ab*
Area = 3,915

_____

3.
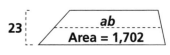
23 *ab*
Area = 1,702

_____

4.
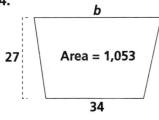
b
27 Area = 1,053
34

_____

5.
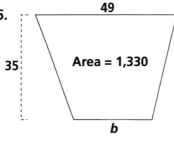
49
35 Area = 1,330
b

_____

6.
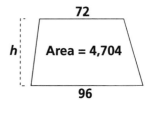
72
h Area = 4,704
96

_____

7.
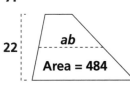
22 *ab*
Area = 484

_____

8.
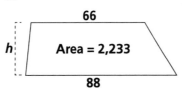
66
h Area = 2,233
88

_____

9.
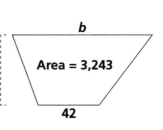
b
47 Area = 3,243
42

_____

10.
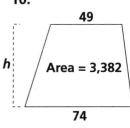
49
h Area = 3,382
74

_____

Heron's Formula

EXAMPLE   Use Heron's Formula to find the area of a triangle with given side lengths. Use a calculator and round to the nearest tenth.

Heron's Formula states that the area of a triangle $= \sqrt{s(s-a)(s-b)(s-c)}$ where $s = \frac{1}{2}(a + b + c)$.

First calculate s. You can write the equation $s = \frac{1}{2}(15 + 19 + 23)$.
This can be simplified to $s = \frac{1}{2}(57) = 28.5$.

Now you can write the equation: area $= \sqrt{28.5(28.5 - 15)(28.5 - 19)(28.5 - 23)}$.

This can be simplified to area $= \sqrt{28.5(13.5)(9.5)(5.5)} \approx \sqrt{20,103.2} \approx 141.8$.

Directions   Use Heron's Formula to find the area of each triangle with the given side lengths. Use a calculator and round to the nearest tenth.

1.
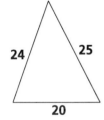
_____

2.
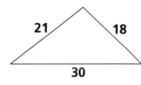
_____

3.
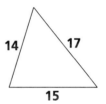
_____

4.
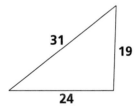
_____

5.
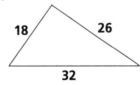
_____

6.
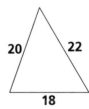
_____

7.
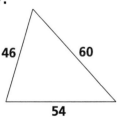
_____

8.
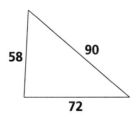
_____

9.
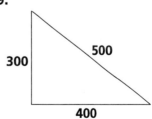
_____

10.
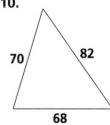
_____

Algebra Connection: Graphing Inequalities

EXAMPLE   Graph the region represented by $y < -x + 4$.

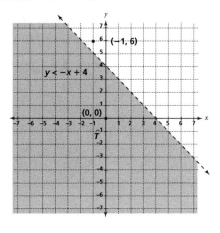

Step 1 Use $y = -x + 4$ and substitution to find two points on the line. Plot the points and draw a broken line between them.

Step 2 Choose two points, one above and one below the line, to see which fulfills the inequality.

$(x, y) = (-1, 6)$	$(x, y) = (0, 0)$
$6 < -(-1) + 4$	$0 < -(0) + 4$
$6 < 5$ False	$0 < 4$ True

Step 3 Shade the region below the broken line. Label the graph.

Directions   Graph these inequalities on a separate sheet of paper.

1. $y > 3x + 2$

2. $y < -\frac{x}{4} + 1$

3. $x > 5$

4. $y > -2x$

5. $x < -1$

EXAMPLE   Graph the region represented by $y \geq \frac{x}{2} - \frac{3}{2}$.

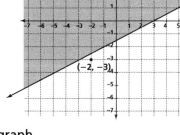

Step 1 Use $y = \frac{x}{2} - \frac{3}{2}$ and substitution to find two points on the line. Plot the points and draw a solid line between them.

Step 2 Choose two points, one above and one below the line, to see which fulfills the inequality.

$(x, y) = (4, 2)$	$(x, y) = (-2, -3)$
$2 \geq \frac{4}{2} - \frac{3}{2}$	$-3 \geq -\frac{2}{2} - \frac{3}{2}$
$2 \geq \frac{1}{2}$ True	$-3 \geq -\frac{5}{2}$ False

Step 3 Shade the region above the solid line. Label the graph.

Directions   Graph these inequalities on a separate sheet of paper.

6. $y \leq -\frac{x}{5} + 5$

7. $x \geq \frac{1}{2}$

8. $y \geq 3x + 4$

9. $y \leq \frac{4}{5}$

10. $x \leq -3$

Definition of a Circle

EXAMPLE The radius of a circle is the distance between the center and any point on the circle. The diameter of a circle is twice as long as the radius of the same circle. The circumference of a circle is 2πr, where r is the radius of the circle.

What is the diameter of the circle with center *X*?   24 units

---

Directions Use the information about radius, diameter, and circumference to answer the following questions. When necessary, write your answer in terms of π.

1. What is the diameter of the circle with center *A*?

_____

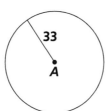

6. What is the circumference of the circle with center *F*?

_____

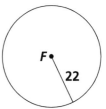

2. What is the diameter of the circle with center *B*?

_____

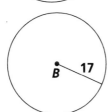

7. What is the radius of the circle with center *G*?

_____

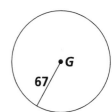

3. What is the radius of the circle with center *C*?

_____

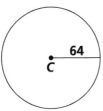

8. What is the diameter of the circle with center *H*?

_____

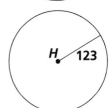

4. What is the circumference of the circle with center *D*?

_____

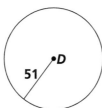

9. What is the circumference of the circle with center *I*?

_____

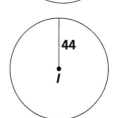

5. What is the diameter of the circle with center *E*?

_____

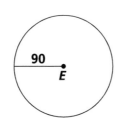

10. What is the diameter of the circle with center *J*?

_____

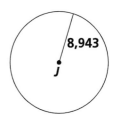

The Ratio π

EXAMPLE   Find the diameter and the radius of a circle with the given circumference.
$C = 66\pi$ in.

The formula for the circumference of a circle is
$C = 2\pi r$, where r equals the radius and C equals the circumference.

$r = \frac{C}{2\pi}$

$r = \frac{66\pi}{2\pi}$

$r = 33$ in.

The diameter of a circle equals two times the radius or $2r$.
Therefore, the diameter of this circle is 66 in.

Directions   Find the diameter and the radius of a circle with the given circumference.

1. $C = 25\pi$ ft   _____ _____

2. $C = 46\pi$ in.   _____ _____

3. $C = 18\pi$ cm   _____ _____

4. $C = 87\pi$ m   _____ _____

5. $C = 65\pi$ mm   _____ _____

6. $C = 28\pi$ ft   _____ _____

7. $C = 78\pi$ in.   _____ _____

8. $C = 32\pi$ cm   _____ _____

9. $C = 20\pi$ m   _____ _____

10. $C = 824\pi$ mm   _____ _____

11. $C = 608\pi$ ft   _____ _____

12. $C = 754\pi$ in.   _____ _____

13. $C = 589\pi$ cm   _____ _____

14. $C = 1,098\pi$ m   _____ _____

15. $C = 5,318\pi$ mm   _____ _____

Approximating the Area of a Circle

EXAMPLE Use the estimation formula to calculate the area of a circle
with the following diameter or radius.

   $r = 3$ units

The estimation formula for the area of a circle is area $\approx 3r^2$.

Write an equation to estimate the area using the above radius.

   area $\approx 3(3)^2$.

This can be simplified to area $\approx 3(9) = 27$ sq units.

Directions Use the estimation formula to calculate the area of a circle
with the following diameter or radius.

1. $d = 12$ _____

2. $r = 12$ _____

3. $d = 24$ _____

4. $r = 13$ _____

5. $d = 40$ _____

6. $d = 60$ _____

7. $r = 8$ _____

8. $r = 19$ _____

9. $d = 64$ _____

10. $r = 25$ _____

Directions Estimate the radius of the circle for the given areas.

11. $A \approx 75$ _____

12. $A \approx 147$ _____

13. $A \approx 243$ _____

14. $A \approx 363$ _____

15. $A \approx 507$ _____

Area and Probability

EXAMPLE	Probability = $\frac{\text{Area of Desired Outcome}}{\text{Total Area}}$

Find the probability of a point being in the shaded area. If you were to draw two segments that connected the opposite midpoints of the rectangle's segments, you would see that the shaded areas of each quarter of the rectangle equal the unshaded areas of each quarter of the rectangle.

Since the amount of shaded area equals the amount of unshaded area, the probability of a point being in the shaded area is 50%.

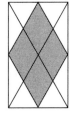

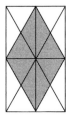

Directions   Find the probability of a point being in the shaded area. Write your answer as a percent.

1.

_____

2.

_____

3.

_____

4.

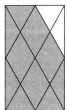

_____

5.

_____

Formula for the Area of a Circle

EXAMPLE   Find the radius of a circle with the given area. Use a calculator and round
the answer to the nearest tenth.

$A = 900$ cm^2

The formula for the area of a circle is $A = \pi r^2$.

You can find the radius by substituting the given area of 900 cm^2 for A in
the equation.

$$900 \text{ cm}^2 = \pi r^2$$

$$\frac{900}{\pi} = r^2$$

$$\sqrt{\frac{900}{\pi}} = r$$

$$16.9 \text{ cm} \approx r$$

Directions   Find the radius of a circle with the given area. Use a calculator and round the
answer to the nearest tenth.

1. $A = 400$ cm^2 _____

2. $A = 876$ cm^2 _____

3. $A = 93$ cm^2 _____

4. $A = 542$ cm^2 _____

5. $A = 650$ cm^2 _____

6. $A = 764$ cm^2 _____

7. $A = 410$ cm^2 _____

8. $A = 999$ cm^2 _____

9. $A = 10{,}000$ cm^2 _____

10. $A = 2{,}340$ cm^2 _____

More Formula for the Area of a Circle

EXAMPLE   Use the formula to find the area. Use a calculator and round the answer to the nearest tenth.

radius = 5.2 in.   diameter = 7 ft

$A = \pi r^2$ $A = \frac{1}{4}\pi d^2$

$A = \pi(5.2)^2$ $A = (\frac{1}{4})\pi(7)^2$

$A = \pi(27.04)$ $A = (\frac{1}{4})\pi(49)$

$A \approx 84.9$ sq in. $A \approx 38.5$ sq ft

Directions   Find the area of a circle with the given radius or diameter. Use a calculator and round the answer to the nearest tenth.

1. $r = 6.4$ in.   _____

2. $r = 9.4$ ft   _____

3. $d = 6.2$ cm   _____

4. $r = 7.4$ units   _____

5. $d = 16$ ft   _____

6. $d = 17$ in.   _____

7. $r = 6.5$ cm   _____

8. $r = 10$ in.   _____

9. $d = 63$ mm   _____

10. $d = 30$ units   _____

Circles and Their Angles and Sectors

EXAMPLE   Find the value of the inscribed angle.

By the theorem, an inscribed angle measures
one half of its intercepted arc.

The intercepted arc measures 90°.

Therefore, the inscribed angle measures $\frac{90}{2}$ = 45°.

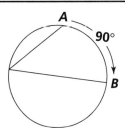

Directions   Find the value of the unknown.

1. inscribed angle

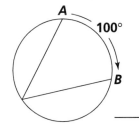

_____

2. arc

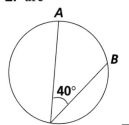

_____

3. inscribed angle

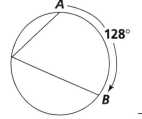

_____

4. arc

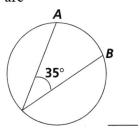

_____

5. inscribed angle

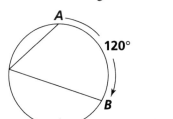

_____

6. arc

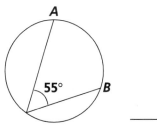

_____

7. inscribed angle

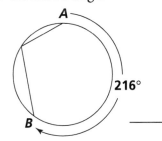

_____

8. arc

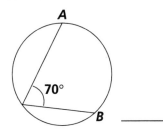

_____

9. inscribed angle

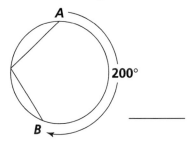

_____

10. arc

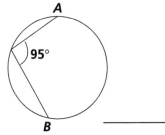

_____

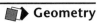

Tangents, Circumcircles, and Incircles

EXAMPLE

What is the largest circle you can fit into △ABC?

The incircle is the largest circle that will fit into △ABC.

To construct the incircle, construct the angle bisectors for two of the triangle's three angles. The point where the bisectors meet will be the center of the incircle. Label this point X.

To find the exact distance of the circle's radius, construct a line that is perpendicular to any side of the triangle that passes through X. Label the point where this perpendicular meets the triangle's side Y. XY is the length of the incircle's radius.

Draw the incircle using X as the center and length XY as the radius.

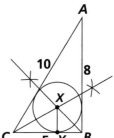

Directions Complete the following constructions on a separate sheet of paper.

1. Construct the incircle for △DEF.

2. Construct the circumcircle for △DEF.

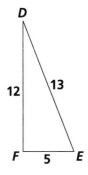

3. Construct the incircle for △XYZ.

4. Construct the circumcircle for △XYZ.

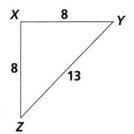

5. Construct the incircle and the circumcircle for △PQR.

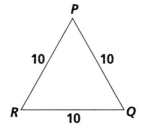

Sine, Cosine, and Tangent

EXAMPLE   Find the sine, cosine, and tangent for angle x.

sine $x = \dfrac{\text{opposite side}}{\text{hypotenuse}}$ sine $x = \dfrac{3}{5} = 0.6$

cosine $x = \dfrac{\text{adjacent side}}{\text{hypotenuse}}$ cosine $x = \dfrac{4}{5} = 0.8$

tangent $x = \dfrac{\text{opposite side}}{\text{adjacent side}}$ tangent $x = \dfrac{3}{4} = 0.75$

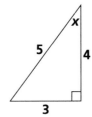

Directions   Find the sine, cosine, and tangent for angle x. Round your answer to the nearest hundredth.

1.
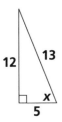

sine   _____

cosine   _____

tangent   _____

4.
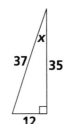

sine   _____

cosine   _____

tangent   _____

2.
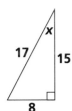

sine   _____

cosine   _____

tangent   _____

5.

sine   _____

cosine   _____

tangent   _____

3.
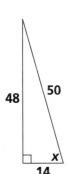

sine   _____

cosine   _____

tangent   _____

Solving Triangles Using Trigonometry

EXAMPLE

Given: right $\triangle ABC$, $m\angle A = 32°$, $AB = 16$

Find: a

$\sin 32° = \frac{a}{16}$ $\qquad$ $16 \cdot \sin 32° = a$

Use a calculator and round to the nearest hundredth.

$a \approx 8.48$

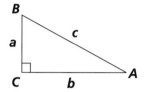

Directions Use right $\triangle ABC$ above. Find a to the nearest hundredth.

1. $m\angle A = 37°$, $AB = 4$ _____

2. $m\angle A = 55°$, $AB = 100$ _____

3. $m\angle A = 29°$, $AB = 30$ _____

4. $m\angle A = 41°$, $AB = 15$ _____

5. $m\angle A = 28°$, $AB = 11$ _____

EXAMPLE

Given: right $\triangle ABC$ above, $m\angle B = 68°$, $BC = 10$

Find: c

$\cos 68° = \frac{10}{c}$ $\qquad$ $c \cdot \cos 68° = 10$ $\qquad$ $c = \frac{10}{\cos 68°}$

Use a calculator and round to the nearest hundredth.

$c \approx 26.69$

Directions Use right $\triangle ABC$ above. Find c to the nearest hundredth.

6. $m\angle B = 63°$, $BC = 90$ _____

7. $m\angle B = 75°$, $BC = 13$ _____

8. $m\angle B = 70°$, $BC = 4$ _____

9. $m\angle B = 80°$, $BC = 44$ _____

10. $m\angle B = 55°$, $BC = 28$ _____

EXAMPLE

Given: right $\triangle ABC$ above, $m\angle A = 20°$, $BC = 15$

Find: b

$\tan 20° = \frac{15}{b}$ $\qquad$ $b \cdot \tan 20° = 15$ $\qquad$ $b = \frac{15}{\tan 20°}$

Use a calculator and round to the nearest hundredth.

$b \approx 41.21$

Directions Use right $\triangle ABC$ above. Find b to the nearest hundredth.

11. $m\angle A = 15°$, $BC = 27$ _____

12. $m\angle A = 39°$, $BC = 10$ _____

13. $m\angle A = 25°$, $BC = 25$ _____

9. $m\angle A = 8°$, $BC = 8$ _____

10. $m\angle A = 12°$, $BC = 30$ _____

Spheres

EXAMPLE   Find the surface area and the volume for a sphere with the given diameter. Use a calculator and round your answer to the nearest hundredth.

$d = 4$

The formula for the surface area of a sphere is $4\pi r^2$. You know that r is the radius and is $\frac{1}{2}$ of the diameter, d. The radius for this sphere is 2.

You can write the equation: surface area = $4\pi(2^2)$.

This can be reduced to: surface area = $4\pi 4 = 16\pi$.

Using your calculator, you can multiply 16 times π and then round to get ≈ 50.27 units^2.

The formula for the volume of a sphere is $\frac{4}{3}\pi r^3$.

You can write the equation: volume = $\frac{4}{3}\pi(2^3)$.

This can be reduced to: volume = $\frac{4}{3}\pi 8 = \frac{32}{3}\pi \approx 33.51$ units^3.

Directions   Find the surface area and the volume of a sphere with the given diameters. Use a calculator and round your answer to the nearest hundredth.

1. $d = 10$ units $S =$ _____ $V =$ _____

2. $d = 6$ units $S =$ _____ $V =$ _____

3. $d = 8$ units $S =$ _____ $V =$ _____

4. $d = 2$ units $S =$ _____ $V =$ _____

5. $d = 14$ units $S =$ _____ $V =$ _____

6. $d = 16$ units $S =$ _____ $V =$ _____

7. $d = 18$ units $S =$ _____ $V =$ _____

8. $d = 20$ units $S =$ _____ $V =$ _____

9. $d = 50$ units $S =$ _____ $V =$ _____

10. $d = 100$ units $S =$ _____ $V =$ _____

Algebra Connection: Systems of Linear Equations

EXAMPLE Find the common solution for $y = 3x - 1$ and $y = x + 3$.
Substitute $x + 3$ for y in $y = 3x - 1$ and solve for x.

$x + 3 = 3x - 1$
$x + 3 - x = 3x - x - 1$ Isolate the variable.
$3 = 2x - 1$
$3 + 1 = 2x - 1 + 1$
$4 = 2x$
$4 \div 2 = 2x \div 2$ Divide out the variable coefficient.
$2 = x$

Substitute 2 for x in either equation. Solve for y.
$y = 2 + 3 = 5$ The common solution is (2, 5).
Check: $3 \cdot 2 - 1 = 6 - 1 = 5$ and $2 + 3 = 5$

Directions   Use substitution to find a common solution. Check your solution.

1. $y = 2x - 3$ and $y = x - 1$ _____   **6.** $y = 4x + 9$ and $y = x + 3$ _____

2. $y = x + 3$ and $y = 4x - 9$ _____   **7.** $y = 11x + 1$ and $y = 3x - 7$ _____

3. $y = -2x - 5$ and $y = x + 1$ _____   **8.** $y = -7x + 9$ and $y = 7x + 23$ _____

4. $y = x - 12$ and $y = -x - 4$ _____   **9.** $y = -x - 7$ and $y = -5x - 3$ _____

5. $y = 3x + 8$ and $y = 2x - 2$ _____   **10.** $y = 7x - 13$ and $y = 6x - 7$ _____

EXAMPLE Find the common solution for $3x - y = 9$ and $x + 2y = 3$.
Multiply $3x - y = 9$ by 2. Add the equations to eliminate y. Solve for x.

$6x - 2y = 18$
$+ \quad x + 2y = 3$
$\overline{7x \qquad = 21} \rightarrow x = 3$

Substitute 3 for x in either equation. Solve for y.
For $x + 2y = 3$, $3 + 2y = 3 \rightarrow y = 0$ The common solution is (3, 0).
Check: $3 \cdot 3 - 0 = 9 - 0 = 9$ and $3 + 2 \cdot 0 = 3 + 0 = 3$

Directions   Use elimination to find a common solution. Check your solution.

11. $3x - y = 1$ and $2x + y = 4$ _____   **16.** $2x - 3y = -30$ and $x + y = 15$ _____

12. $2x - y = -1$ and $x + y = 4$ _____   **17.** $-x - y = 1$ and $5x + 2y = -11$ _____

13. $-x + y = 5$ and $3x - y = 3$ _____   **18.** $-2x + y = -2$ and $x + 3y = -6$ _____

14. $-x - 5y = -3$ and $x + y = 7$ _____   **19.** $x + 2y = 7$ and $-6x + y = 10$ _____

15. $4x + 5y = 13$ and $-4x + y = -7$ _____   **20.** $-x - y = 2$ and $6x + 5y = -3$ _____

Basic Volume Formulas

EXAMPLE	The formula for the volume of a rectangular solid is $V = l \cdot w \cdot h$ or $v =$ (base area) $\cdot$ (height). You are given a value of 24,000 for V, 20 for l, and 40 for w.

Write the equation $24{,}000 = 20 \cdot 40 \cdot x$, to solve for x. This can be reduced to $24{,}000 = 800 \cdot x$. Divide both sides by 800 to get $x = 30$.

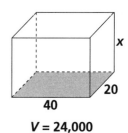

$V = 24{,}000$

Directions   Use what you know about volume to find the unknown.

1.
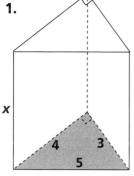

$V = 30$ _____

2.
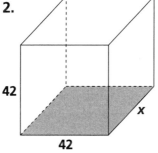

$V = 74{,}088$ _____

3.
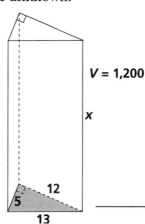

$V = 1{,}200$

_____

4.
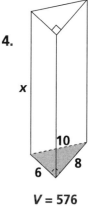

$V = 576$

_____

5.
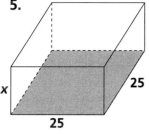

$V = 7{,}500$ _____

6.
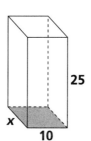

$V = 2{,}500$ _____

7.
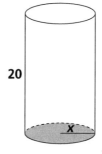

$V = 2{,}260.8$

8.
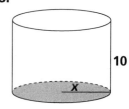

$V = 1{,}538.6$

_____

9.
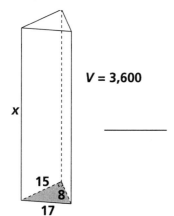

$V = 3{,}600$

_____

10.
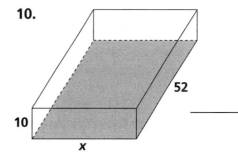

$V = 18{,}720$

Volumes of Pyramids and Cones

EXAMPLE   Find the volume of the following cone.

The formula for the volume of a cone or pyramid is:
$V = \frac{1}{3}$(area of base)(height).

You are given a value of 3 for the radius of the base. Calculate the area of
the base using the formula for the area of a circle, area = πr^2.

Write an equation for the area of the base, area = $\pi 3^2$. This can be
simplified to: area = $\pi 9 \approx 28.3$.

Write an equation for the volume of the cone,
$V = \frac{1}{3}$(area of base)(height) $\approx \frac{1}{3}$(28.3)(9) = 84.9.

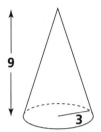

Directions   Find the volume of each pyramid or cone. When necessary, round your
answer to the nearest tenth.

1.

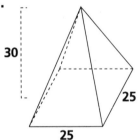

30   25
25

_____

2.

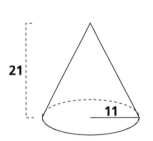

21   11

_____

3.

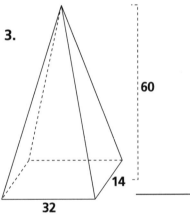

60   14
32

_____

4.

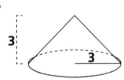

3   3

_____

5.

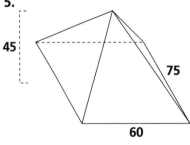

45   75
60

_____

Surface Areas of Prisms and Cylinders

EXAMPLE
The formula for the surface area of a rectangular prism is

$$SA = 2(lw + hl + hw).$$

You are given values of 5, 7, and 6 for *l*, *w*, and *h*.

Write the equation $SA = 2((5\cdot7)+(5\cdot6)+(6\cdot7))$. This can be reduced to
$SA = 2(35 + 30 + 42) = 2(107) = 214.$

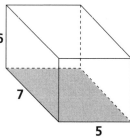

Directions Find the surface area of each of the following three-dimensional figures. Round your answer to the nearest hundredth.

1. 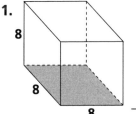 8, 8, 8

2. 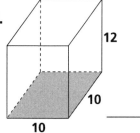 12, 10, 10

3. 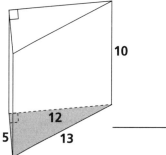 10, 12, 5, 13

4. 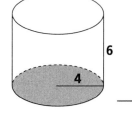 6, 4

5. 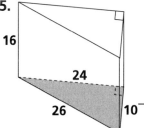 16, 24, 26, 10

6. 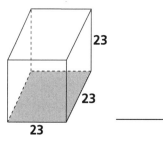 23, 23, 23

7. 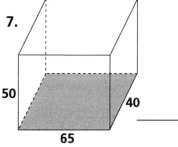 50, 40, 65

8. 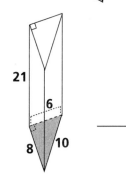 21, 6, 8, 10

9. 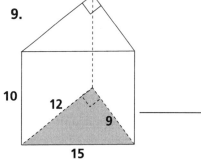 10, 12, 9, 15

10. 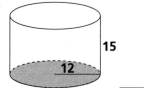 15, 12

Surface Areas of Pyramids and Cones

EXAMPLE | Find the surface area of this pyramid. The formula for the surface area of a pyramid is *SA* = area of base + area of four triangles.

$$SA = (s \bullet s) + \tfrac{1}{2}sl + \tfrac{1}{2}sl + \tfrac{1}{2}sl + \tfrac{1}{2}sl = s^2 + 2sl \text{ where}$$
l is the measure of the slant height.

You are given a value of 15 for *s* and a value of 10 for *l*.

Write the equation *SA* = 15² + 2(15 • 10).
This can be simplified to *SA* = 225 + 300 = 525.

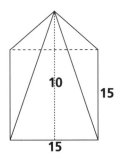

Directions Find the surface area of these pyramids and cones. Round your answer to the nearest hundredth.

1.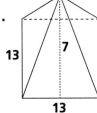

13 7 13

_____

2.

7 4

_____

3.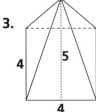

4 5 4

_____

4.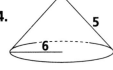

5 6

_____

5.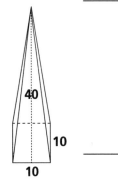

40 10 10

_____

6.

5 9

_____

7.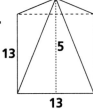

13 5 13

_____

8.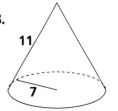

11 7

_____

9.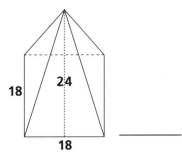

18 24 18

_____

10.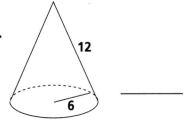

12 6

_____

Measurements

EXAMPLE   Complete the following statement.

14 pints = ____ gallons

You know that 1 gallon equals 4 quarts. You also know that 1 quart equals 2 pints. Therefore, 1 gallon = 4 quarts = 8 pints.

If you substitute 8 pints for gallons, you can write the following equation.

14 pints = x(8 pints). Divide both sides by 8 pints to get x = 1.75 gallons.

Directions   Complete each statement.

1. 5 ft = _____ in.

2. 13 yd = _____ ft

3. 56 in. = _____ ft

4. 7 mi = _____ yd

5. 58,080 ft = _____ mi

6. 78 gallons = _____ qt

7. 28 cups = _____ pints

8. 304 ounces = _____ lb

9. 15 cups = _____ fl oz

10. 90,000 lb = _____ tons

11. 66 kg = _____ g

12. 57 L = _____ mL

13. 92 cm = _____ mm

14. 843 cm = _____ m

15. 88 km = _____ cm

16. 85 ft = _____ in.

17. 36 yd = _____ ft

18. 1,008 in. = _____ ft

19. 12 mi = _____ yd

20. 290,400 ft = _____ mi

Algebra Connection: Radicals in Equations

EXAMPLE   Solve for x when $\sqrt{x+4} = 3$.
Square both sides of the equation and solve.
$(\sqrt{x+4})^2 = 3^2 \rightarrow x + 4 = 9 \rightarrow x = 5$
Check: $\sqrt{5+4} = \sqrt{9} = 3$

Directions   Solve for x. Check your work.

1. $\sqrt{4x} = 2$ _____

2. $\sqrt{5x} = 5$ _____

3. $\sqrt{3x} = 6$ _____

4. $\sqrt{6x} = 3$ _____

5. $\sqrt{x-3} = 1$ _____

6. $\sqrt{x+9} = 3$ _____

7. $\sqrt{x-6} = 0$ _____

8. $\sqrt{x-5} = 3$ _____

9. $\sqrt{x+10} = 2$ _____

10. $\sqrt{x-9} = 15$ _____

11. $\sqrt{x-12} = 6$ _____

12. $-\sqrt{x+8} = -6$ _____

13. $-\sqrt{x+18} = -2$ _____

14. $-\sqrt{x-5} = -2$ _____

15. $\sqrt{2x+1} = 3$ _____

EXAMPLE   Solve for x when $8 - \sqrt{7x} = 1$.
$8 - \sqrt{7x} - 8 = 1 - 8$ Get the variable term by itself.
$-\sqrt{7x} = -7$
Square both sides of the equation and solve.
$(-\sqrt{7x})^2 = (-7)^2 \rightarrow 7x = 49 \rightarrow x = 7$
Check: $8 - \sqrt{7 \cdot 7} = 8 - 7 = 1$

Directions   Solve for x. Check your work.

16. $5 + \sqrt{2x} = 9$ _____

17. $7 - \sqrt{7x} = 0$ _____

18. $8 + \sqrt{3x} = 14$ _____

19. $6 - \sqrt{4x} = 2$ _____

20. $2 - \sqrt{7x} = -5$ _____

21. $3 - \sqrt{8x} = -9$ _____

22. $5 + \sqrt{4x} = 13$ _____

23. $4 + \sqrt{6x} = 6$ _____

24. $-6 + \sqrt{9x} = 6$ _____

25. $2 + \sqrt{3x} = 4$ _____

26. $4 - \sqrt{4x} = 3$ _____

27. $3 + \sqrt{x-1} = 7$ _____

28. $4 + \sqrt{x+1} = 6$ _____

29. $-3 + \sqrt{2x-1} = 4$ _____

30. $8 - \sqrt{2x+1} = 3$ _____

Lines and Planes in Space

EXAMPLE   Review the following.

A line that does not intersect an object shares no points
in common with it.

A line that is tangent to an object
touches it at only one point.

A line that intersects an object at two points crosses
the object but does not run along its surface.

A line that shares a segment of its points with an object runs
along the object's surface.

Directions   Given a plane and a cube in space, draw a sketch of and then
describe the following. Use a separate sheet of paper.

1. The plane and the cube have one point in common.

2. The plane and the cube share a segment of points in common.

3. The plane and the cube share the perimeter of a square in common.

4. The plane and the cube share the area of a square in common.

5. The plane and the cube share no points in common.

Loci in the Coordinate Plane

| **EXAMPLE** | Find the loci of points 2 units from the origin. Draw a sketch and write the equation. |

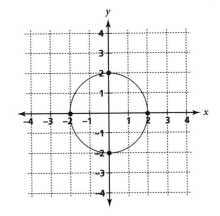

You know that the locus of points equidistant from one point forms a circle with a radius that is equal to the distance given. Therefore, the locus of points 2 units from the origin will form a circle with the origin as the center and a radius of 2. You can draw this using a compass, as shown.

You know that the formula for a circle with radius r and center $(0, 0)$ is $r^2 = x^2 + y^2$. Therefore, the equation for this circle is $2^2 = x^2 + y^2$. This can be simplified to $4 = x^2 + y^2$.

Directions Find the locus. Draw a sketch on a separate sheet of paper. Then write the equation.

1. Loci of points 7 units from the origin   _____

2. Loci of points 8 units from the origin   _____

3. Loci of points 9 units from the origin   _____

4. Loci of points 10 units from the origin   _____

5. Loci of points 20 units from the origin   _____

Compound Loci

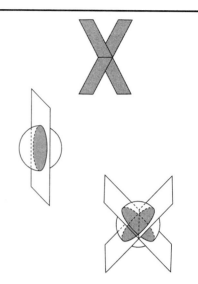

| EXAMPLE | Sketch, then describe, the following compound locus: The intersection of two planes and a sphere where each plane crosses the sphere to form a great circle. |

You know that the intersection of two planes forms a line. You also know that in order for a great circle to be formed by the intersection of a plane and a sphere, the plane must pass through the circle's center.

In order for both planes to cross each other and form great circles with the sphere, the line formed by the crossing planes must pass through the sphere's center.

Directions   Sketch and describe the following compound loci.

1. The intersection of a triangular prism with a plane where the plane crosses through the side of one of the bases and a vertex of the other base

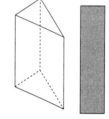

2. The intersection of a triangle-based pyramid and a plane that is parallel with the base of the pyramid

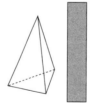

3. The intersection of an ellipse-based cone and a plane where the plane is parallel with the base

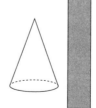

4. The intersection of a plane and a cone where the plane is perpendicular to the base and passes through the point of the cone

5. The intersection of a cone and a plane in which the plane is not parallel with the base but does intersect the base

Algebra Connection: The Quadratic Formula

EXAMPLE   Write the equation of the axis of symmetry for $y = 2x^2 - 8x + 3$.

Are the roots real or complex?

The equation is in the form $y = ax^2 + bx + c$.

The equation of the axis of symmetry is $x = -\frac{b}{2a}$.

Substitute 2 for a and -8 for b. $x = -\frac{-8}{2 \cdot 2} = \frac{8}{4} = 2 \rightarrow x = 2$

Substitute 2 for a, -8 for b, and 3 for c to find if $b^2 - 4ac > 0$ or < 0.

$b^2 - 4ac = (-8)^2 - 4 \cdot (2) \cdot (3) = 64 - 24 = 40$

$40 > 0$, so $2x^2 - 8x + 3 = 0$ has two real roots.

If $b^2 - 4ac = 0$, however, the equation has one real root.

Directions   Write the equation of the line of symmetry. Are the roots real or complex?

1. $y = x^2 - x - 3$ _____

2. $y = x^2 + 4x + 4$ _____

3. $y = -2x^2 + x + 7$ _____

4. $y = 5x^2 + 4x - 1$ _____

5. $y = 4x^2 - 7x + 5$ _____

6. $y = 2x^2 - x + 4$ _____

7. $y = x^2 - 3x - 8$ _____

8. $y = 7x^2 + 5x - 1$ _____

9. $y = -x^2 + 3x + 6$ _____

10. $y = 3x^2 + 8x + 4$ _____

EXAMPLE   Find the roots of the equation $3x^2 = 4x + 7$.

Rewrite the equation in standard form. $3x^2 - 4x - 7 = 0$

Substitute 3 for a, -4 for b, and -7 for c in the quadratic formula.

$$x = \frac{-b \pm \sqrt{b^2 - 4ac}}{2a} = \frac{-(-4) \pm \sqrt{(-4)^2 - 4 \cdot (3)(-7)}}{2 \cdot 3} = 4 \pm \frac{\sqrt{16 + 84}}{6} = \frac{4 \pm \sqrt{100}}{6} = \frac{4 \pm 10}{6}$$

$$x = \frac{4 + 10}{6} = \frac{14}{6} = \frac{7}{3} \quad \text{or} \quad \frac{4 - 10}{6} = \frac{-6}{6} = -1$$

Check: $3 \cdot (\frac{7}{3})^2 = 3 \cdot \frac{49}{9} = \frac{49}{3}$ and $4 \cdot (\frac{7}{3}) + 7 = \frac{28}{3} + \frac{21}{3} = \frac{49}{3}$

$3 \cdot (-1)^2 = 3$ and $4 \cdot (-1) + 7 = -4 + 7 = 3$ Both solutions check.

Directions   Solve for x. Check your answers.

11. $x^2 - 2x - 3 = 0$ _____

12. $x^2 - 8x + 15 = 0$ _____

13. $5x^2 - x - 6 = 0$ _____

14. $2x^2 - x - 3 = 0$ _____

15. $2x^2 + 6x + 4 = 0$ _____

16. $-2x^2 + 9x = 7$ _____

17. $5x^2 = -x + 6$ _____

18. $3x^2 - 8x = -4$ _____

19. $2x^2 + 5x = 18$ _____

20. $4x^2 + 2x = 6$ _____

Axioms, Postulates, and Theorems

Axioms

Axiom 1 Things that are equal to the same thing are equal to each other.

Axiom 2 If equals are added to equals, the sums are equal.

Axiom 3 If equals are subtracted from equals, the differences are equal.

Axiom 4 Things that are alike or coincide with one another are equal to one another.

Axiom 5 The whole, or sum, is greater than the parts.

Postulates

Ruler Postulate The points on a line can be placed in a one-to-one correspondence with the real numbers so that

1. for every point on the line, there is exactly one real number.

2. for every real number, there is exactly one point on the line.

3. the distance between any two points is the absolute value of the difference of the corresponding real numbers.

Ruler Placement Postulate Given two points, A and B on a line, the number line can be chosen so that A is at zero and B is at a positive number.

Segment Addition Postulate If B is between A and C, then $AB + BC = AC$.

Euclid's Postulate 1 A straight line can be drawn from any point to any point.

Euclid's Postulate 2 A finite straight line can be extended continuously in a straight line.

Euclid's Postulate 3 A circle may be described with any center and distance.

Axioms, Postulates, and Theorems

Euclid's Postulate 4 All right angles are equal to one another.

Euclid's Postulate 5 If two lines ℓ and m are cut by a third line t, and the two inside angles, a and b, together measure less than two right angles, then the two lines ℓ and m, if extended, will meet on the same side of t as the two angles a and b.

Parallel Postulate 5 If there is a line ℓ and a point P not on ℓ, then there is only one line that passes through P and is parallel to ℓ.

Alternate Interior Angles Postulate If a transversal intersects two lines so that the alternate interior angles are equal, then the lines are parallel.

SAS (Side-Angle-Side) Postulate If two sides and the included angle of one triangle are congruent to the corresponding two sides and included angle of a second triangle, the triangles are congruent.

SSS (Side-Side-Side) Postulate If three sides of a triangle are congruent to three sides of a second triangle, then the triangles are congruent.

ASA (Angle-Side-Angle) Postulate If two angles and the included side of a triangle are congruent to the corresponding angles and included side of a second triangle, then the triangles are congruent.

AA Similarity Postulate If two angles of a triangle have the same measures as two angles of a second triangle, then the two triangles are similar.

Theorems

Vertical Angle Theorem (2.5.1) If angles are vertical angles, then their measures are equal.

Theorem 3.3.1 If two lines are parallel, then the interior angles on the same side of the transversal are supplementary.

Theorem 3.3.2 If two lines cut by a transversal are parallel, then the corresponding angles are equal.

Theorem 3.3.3 If two lines cut by a transversal are parallel, then the alternate interior angles are equal.

Theorem 3.5.1 If a figure is a parallelogram, then its angle sum is 360°.

Theorem 3.6.1 If a figure is a trapezoid, then its angle sum is 360°.

Theorem 3.7.1 If corresponding angles are equal, then the lines are parallel.

Theorem 3.8.1 If two lines are cut by a transversal so that the angles on the same side of the transversal are supplementary, then the lines are parallel.

Theorem 5.4.1 In rectangle $ABCD$ with diagonal $\overline{AC}$, $m\angle 1 = m\angle 4$ and $m\angle 2 = m\angle 3$.

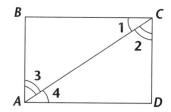

Angle Sum Theorem (5.9.1) The sum of the angle measures in any triangle is 180°.

Corollary to the Angle Sum Theorem (5.9.2) If $\triangle ABC$ is any triangle, then an exterior angle of ABC has the same measure as the sum of the measures of the two nonadjacent interior angles.

Shortest Distance Theorem (6.2.1) The perpendicular segment from a point to a line is the shortest segment from that point to the line. The length of the perpendicular segment is called the *distance* from the point to the line.

Triangle Inequality Theorem (6.2.2) The sum of the lengths of any two sides of a triangle must be greater than the length of the third side.

AAS (Angle-Angle-Side) Theorem (6.4.1) If two angles and one side not included between those angles are congruent to two angles and the corresponding side of a second triangle, then the two triangles are congruent.

Theorem 6.4.2 The acute angles in any right triangle are complementary.

Hypotenuse-Leg (H-L) Theorem (6.4.3) Two right triangles are congruent if the hypotenuse and leg of one triangle are congruent to the hypotenuse and corresponding leg of the second triangle.

Theorem 7.1.1 In any proportion, the product of the extremes equals the product of the means.

Theorem 7.2.1 If one acute angle of a right triangle has the same measure as one acute angle of a second right triangle, then the two right triangles are similar.

Pythagorean Theorem (8.2.1) If a triangle is a right triangle with legs a and b and hypotenuse c, then $a^2 + b^2 = c^2$.

(8.4.1) In any right triangle ABC, with hypotenuse $\overline{AC}$, $(AC)^2 = (AB)^2 + (BC)^2$.

Theorem 8.5.1 The angles opposite equal sides in a triangle are equal.

Theorem 8.5.2 In a 30°-60° right triangle, the side opposite the 30° angle is one-half the length of the hypotenuse.

Converse of the Pythagorean Theorem (8.8.1) If for $\triangle ABC$, $(AC)^2 = (AB)^2 + (BC)^2$, then $\triangle ABC$ is a right triangle.

Theorem 10.6.1 The measure of an inscribed angle is half the measure of its intercepted arc.